READING
AT GREATER
DEPTH
→ IN KEY STAGE TWO ←

READING
AT GREATER
DEPTH

→ IN KEY STAGE TWO ←

SUZANNE HORTON
LOUISE BEATTIE
SHARON LANNIE

SAGE | Learning Matters

Learning Matters
An imprint of SAGE Publications Ltd
1 Oliver's Yard
55 City Road
London EC1Y 1SP

SAGE Publications Inc.
2455 Teller Road
Thousand Oaks, California 91320

SAGE Publications India Pvt Ltd
B 1/I 1 Mohan Cooperative Industrial Area
Mathura Road
New Delhi 110 044

SAGE Publications Asia-Pacific Pte Ltd
3 Church Street
#10-04 Samsung Hub
Singapore 049483

Editor: Amy Thornton
Development editor: Geoff Barker
Senior project editor: Chris Marke
Project management: Deer Park Productions, Tavistock
Marketing manager: Catherine Slinn
Cover design: Wendy Scott
Typeset by: C&M Digitals (P) Ltd, Chennai, India
Printed in the UK

First published in 2019 by Learning Matters Ltd

© 2019 Suzanne Horton, Louise Beattie and
Sharon Lannie

Library of Congress Control Number: 2018957322

British Library Cataloguing in Publication Data

A catalogue record for this book is available from the
British Library

ISBN: 978 1 5264 4169 0
ISBN: 978 1 5264 4170 6 (pbk)

At SAGE we take sustainability seriously. Most of our products are printed in the UK using responsibly sourced
papers and boards. When we print overseas we ensure sustainable papers are used as measured by the PREPS
grading system. We undertake an annual audit to monitor our sustainability.

CONTENTS

PERMISSIONS

Every effort has been made to trace the copyright holders and to obtain their permission for the use of copyright material. The publisher and author will gladly receive any information enabling them to rectify any error or omission in subsequent editions.

THE AUTHORS

Suzanne Horton is Course Leader for the BA (Hons) Primary Initial Teacher Education degree at the University of Worcester and teaches on a range of postgraduate and undergraduate modules. Suzanne taught English in a range of primary schools for over twenty years and became an Advanced Skills Teacher supporting the teaching of English in a variety of schools, and regularly spends time in schools, working with children. She is currently engaged in research around the teaching of early reading and also exploring the transition between primary and secondary school.

Louise Beattie is the subject lead for the PGCE Secondary English course at the University of Worcester. For twenty years previously, she worked in a range of secondary schools in a variety of roles. She has worked at Head of Department level and spent ten years working as an English Adviser in a local authority. This afforded her the opportunity of working in a wide array of secondary schools, special schools and primary schools. Her teaching interests include the teaching of speaking and listening and their links to writing and how explicit teacher commentary can enhance learning. Current research includes pupil transition from Key Stage 2 to 3.

Sharon Lannie is module leader for PGCE English at the University of Worcester. She supports the development of English in schools through leading a termly network meeting for primary and middle school English subject leaders across Worcestershire and beyond. For twenty years, Sharon taught English in primary and middle schools across Worcestershire and overseas, has been the English co-ordinator in three different schools and has worked as a lead teacher for English with the local authority.

THE AUTHORS

1
READING AT GREATER DEPTH

Reading

The more that you read, the more things you will know.

The more that you learn, the more places you'll go.

(Dr Seuss, *I Can Read With My Eyes Shut!*)

Reading is a multi-layered experience which necessitates interaction with print in order to extract meaning. It draws upon a number of skills: being able to recognise letters, match letters to sounds and then blending phonemes to formulate words. It also demands an understanding of sentence structure, the meanings of words and the world around us to fully engage with the author's intent. Those readers who are able to use context to help read new and unfamiliar words will demonstrate greater understanding. It is important that we, as the class teacher, nurture this practice and continue to challenge our pupils by facilitating access to texts which allow for the development of higher-level thinking. By reading widely, children will extend their reading repertoire and develop those higher-level skills of analysis, criticality and evaluation – while also increasing their knowledge and understanding of the world and society as a whole.

What do we mean by a 'higher-level reader'?

Throughout this book, we outline many ways to develop readers and challenge thinking. Reading at a 'higher level', 'developing mastery within reading', 'extending thinking' and 'reading at greater depth' are all terms with which we are becoming familiar but what does this look like in terms of learning gain for pupils and how do we define a 'higher-level reader'?

If we start with the discussion around what might be considered reading at an advanced level, we can begin to explore the various ideas and opinions that surround this concept. This is somewhat problematic as a survey of the literature around higher-level readers suggests that there is no one definition (Brighton *et al.*, 2015). However, there is some consensus as to the attributes one might expect a higher-level reader to demonstrate. These include a more sophisticated vocabulary development, an enjoyment of reading, the ability to analyse, evaluate and synthesise effectively together with the ability to be critical yet creative in their approach to texts (Reis *et al.*, 2004). Reiss *et al.* also cite advanced language skills as an important characteristic of an advanced reader which suggests the importance of the social aspect of reading. Reading is not a solitary activity but one which demands that we discuss ideas, challenge each other in terms of knowledge held, argue, debate and rationalise our thoughts. Indeed, according to Cremin *et al.* (2014, p5) *the act of reading remains profoundly social*. If we also consider Aidan Chambers' work around 'Booktalk', the importance of being able to articulate thoughts and co-construct knowledge through a shared response is another obvious indicator of a higher level of reading. As teachers, we must enable our pupils to become advanced readers by providing opportunities to build the aforementioned characteristics while teaching the skills to achieve this. The following chapters will examine the rationale behind this approach and offer some practical teaching, learning and assessment strategies to develop this effectively within your own classroom.

CASE STUDY: TOM – AN ADVANCED READER

Tom is a Year 6 pupil, looking forward to transitioning to high school at the end of the year. His teacher has categorised him as an advanced reader, based on teacher assessment, his SATs reading score and her knowledge of Tom as a reader. While success in statutory tests should not and does not define a 'good' reader, Tom's teacher had worked extensively with a group of higher-level readers to develop and extend their comprehension skills throughout the year and was able to identify the characteristics which suggested that he was working at greater depth. These included:

- a wide and varied vocabulary – Tom understood the nuances of language and was able to draw upon an expansive vocabulary to articulate his point;
- an ability to explain what words meant and offer synonyms as alternatives;
- an understanding of the subtleties of humour within texts and being able to comment on authorial intent;
- being able to use a range of inference skills across a wide variety of genres;
- making insightful predictions based on what had been read;
- the ability to visualise the scene, making links between what was stated and what was implied in order to have the overall picture;
- effective analysis of texts based on information within the text and making links between events;
- evaluation of the significance of events within a text from different perspectives;
- an acute understanding of characters' motives and actions;
- the ability to ask questions of the text in order to extend understanding;
- an obvious love of reading.

When asked what made him such a good reader, he explained that he had access to many books at home and at school, enjoyed opportunities to talk about what he was reading with peers and adults and loved learning new words.

We know from research that a good level of vocabulary contributes positively to reading comprehension (Clarke *et al.*, 2010) and that young people who read for pleasure demonstrate higher attainment (Clark and Teravainen, 2017). The positive classroom environment that Tom's class teacher had cultivated almost certainly contributed to his success in reading. However, it is important to acknowledge that not all homes have access to books in the same way that Tom did, therefore it is imperative that class teachers find ways to ensure their classroom library is fully stocked and that links with local libraries remain strong. With the decrease in school budgets and the demise of local libraries, it is easy to become disheartened when trying to maintain a comprehensive reading area. Twitter provides an excellent forum for connecting with authors, charities and proponents of reading in order to replenish stocks. You could also visit charity shops and second-hand book shops for a wide and varied range of children's books. Book swaps work successfully in school as does the sharing of online texts which can reduce the need to purchase multiple copies of texts. Building partnerships with other local schools or connecting via Twitter may lead to class sets being swapped at different times of the year. Be creative!

Reading comprehension

The following section will provide an overview of what we mean by reading comprehension and why it is important in developing and challenging readers.

RESEARCH FOCUS: APPROACHES TO READING

Lambirth (2011) outlines three approaches that have been influential in shaping educational policy over a number of decades. These theoretical models explore how reading can be taught and its effect upon comprehension. Through examining each approach, we are able to develop an understanding of the ways in which we can support pupils to enhance their comprehension skills. While common sense tells us that there is no 'one size fits all' panacea when teaching reading, there are elements of each theoretical model that may enhance practice. How does your classroom environment reflect each of the approaches?

The cognitive-psychological approach (CPA)

This is what may be termed as a 'bottom-up' approach to reading whereby readers start with the way in which sounds are represented, building up to words, sentences and then texts. There is a focus on grapho-phonic cueing systems rather than contextual clues. Word identification is key within this approach and proponents of this method suggest that comprehension skills will be developed more effectively and more quickly through explicit instruction in decoding than by employing other approaches. Phonics – first and fast – has been synonymous with this approach as advocated by the Rose Review (Rose, 2006) with its emphasis on systematic synthetic phonics. While this is a much contested approach to reading, it dominates current educational policy.

The psycholinguistic approach

Ken Goodman is perhaps the most well-known academic associated with this approach. Sometimes known as the whole language approach, the psycholinguistic approach suggests that children have an innate ability to make meaning and should enhance this through authentic experiences. Rather than a series of skills to be taught, reading is seen as a holistic process which draws upon three cueing strategies to make meaning: semantic cues (making meaning), grapho-phonic cues (GPCs) and syntactic cues (grammatical structures), and may be best represented as in Figure 1.1 below.

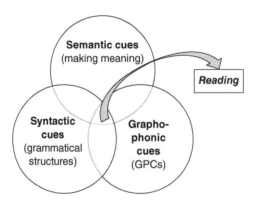

Figure 1.1   Cueing strategies for reading (Horton et al., 2015)

The sociocultural approach

Reading is seen much more as taking place within a sociocultural environment where the reader is an active constructor of their own learning. It requires active participation and interaction with others therefore is not achieved through explicit technical instruction. According to Gee, a leading expert on the sociocultural approach to learning to read, children learn more effectively within a meaningful and purposeful context (Gee, 2004). A range of literacies are valued within the classroom as they have an impact upon developing reading and comprehension for the individual.

Guppy and Hughes (1999) outlined three levels of comprehension, each one necessary to derive meaning from the text:

- *Reading the lines* – meaning is made from what is explicitly stated in the text. It is the literal interpretation.

- *Reading between the lines* – the reader must infer meaning based on what is implied within the text.

- *Reading beyond the lines* – meaning is developed through reacting to the text and evaluating this with reference to the feelings that the author has evoked. It is an appreciation of the author's craft.

So, what does this look like in practice? Read the following extract taken from *The Explorer* by Katherine Rundell and answer the questions below.

It was ferociously hot, and he was still alive. Those were the first thoughts that came to Fred as he opened his eyes and found himself staring straight up at the Brazilian sun. Instinctively he looked down at his wristwatch, but the face was cracked and the minute hand had fallen off.

(Rundell, 2017)

- Where is Fred?
- What do you think may have happened?
- Why is it important that we know his watch has broken?

The first question is a closed question which requests information that is stated in the text. Answers may include Brazil, somewhere hot, another country.

Question two requires the reader to read a little more deeply into the text in order to answer. There is no definitive answer although the reader must use the clues from the text and their own knowledge and experience of the world to make an informed contribution. We start by inferring that the pronoun 'it' in the first sentence refers to the weather, the climate or the atmosphere. This cohesive device allows us to construct a meaningful representation of the situation. Knowledge-based inferences rely on the reader's experiences and understanding of the world therefore we have to know that by stating that 'he was still alive' means that something has happened whereby he might have died – this leads us to infer that Fred may be in a

(Continued)

(Continued)

dangerous situation. What we are doing is bridging the gap between what is stated and what is implied. There are a number of possibilities as to what may have happened and, through discussion with other readers, pupils will begin to refine their ideas as they explore the incidents that may have led to this situation. Discussions are beneficial as they allow children to re-think, re-shape and extend their ideas in light of other opinions. It is this critical thinking that defines an effective reader.

The last question is more demanding in terms of comprehension as it requires the reader to examine the significance of this sentence within a wider context – we are looking at the bigger picture. We are able to question the inclusion of this sentence within the extract and examine the reasons why the author has informed us of this at this particular moment in the narrative. This is a non-literal interpretation and relies on the reader connecting information within the text with their knowledge of the world: through identifying the watch as having symbolic meaning it is almost as if time has stopped still due to the magnitude of the situation in which Fred finds himself.

Children may begin to wonder why Fred is on his own or where his parents are. They may start to predict what might happen next or want to know more about Fred and his predicament. They may choose to ask why the author has used the word 'instinctively'? What does this tell us about the character, the situation? From a collection of three sentences and three questions, we have provided the reader with an opportunity to extend their thinking, articulate their views and apply prior knowledge – all attributes of a 'higher-level reader'.

Developing high-level reading skills: the challenge

There are a number of challenges when developing high-level reading skills with children which need to be explored in order to be able to effectively address this within the classroom. Some of these have already been explored above.

Challenging texts

As previously stated, not all schools and pupils have access to an endless supply of good quality texts although solutions have been proposed as part of Tom's case study. This is further compounded by a lack of texts which are challenging yet age appropriate in terms of content. According to Shanahan *et al.*, *just as it's impossible to build muscle without weight or resistance, it's impossible to build robust reading skills without reading challenging text* (Shanahan *et al.*, 2012, p52). The importance of providing challenging texts is crucial in continuing to enhance comprehension skills and so these should be chosen wisely. According to Fang and Pace (2013), text difficulty may be determined through the application of five linguistic sources of complexity:

- *vocabulary* – the inclusion of more complex vocabulary: tier 2 or 3 words (Beck *et al.*, 2013);
- *grammatical metaphors* – atypical ways of representing meaning which can be abstract;
- *cohesion* – where sentences do not link explicitly and there may be ambiguity;

- *lexical density* – a prevalence of content words with a number of expanded noun phrases;

- *grammatical intricacy* – long, complex sentences with multiple clauses.

Complexity may also be determined through the themes that are introduced and the level of criticality necessary to fully explore the text. This is examined in more detail in Chapter 9. The only successful way of knowing the right texts to use is by reading the text before introducing it to your class and by knowing your pupils and their backgrounds. You, as the teacher, are best placed to judge the suitability of content and themes.

Ten challenging texts for developing high-level comprehension skills:

Where the World Ends by Geraldine McCaughrean

Lord of the Rings by JRR Tolkien

Skellig by David Almond

Sky Song by Abi Elphinstone

Beyond the Bright Sea by Lauren Wolk

La Belle Sauvage: The Book of Dust Volume One by Philip Pullman

Welcome to Nowhere by Elizabeth Laird

Animal Farm by George Orwell

The Coral Island by RM Ballantyne

Small Steps by Louis Sachar

The national curriculum

Throughout this book, there are numerous references to the national curriculum with reference to statutory requirements and the programmes of study. If we look closely at the expectations for upper Key Stage 2, we can clearly see the scope of learning that should be evident in order to develop comprehension skills and prepare pupils to be 'secondary ready'.

Pupils should be taught to:

- understand what they read, in books they can read independently, by:
  - o checking that the text makes sense to them, discussing their understanding and explaining the meaning of words in context;
  - o asking questions to improve their understanding of a text;
  - o drawing inferences such as inferring characters' feelings, thoughts and motives from their actions, and justifying those inferences with evidence;

o   predicting what might happen from details stated and implied;

o   identifying main ideas drawn from more than one paragraph and summarising these;

o   identifying how language, structure and presentation contribute to meaning.

(DfE, 2013)

Vocabulary development, explanation, analysis, prediction, reasoning, justifying, summarising and presenting are all key skills outlined above. Through the implementation of successful reading programmes, pupils will develop comprehension skills effectively. The challenge for teachers lies with unpicking the objectives above so as to ensure manageable steps of progression for readers while ensuring coverage of the content domains, the areas of reading that are tested on the SATs papers for Key Stage 2. These were not introduced as a replacement for the previous assessment focuses, nor are they intended to replace the content in the national curriculum. By using these to underpin the teaching of reading while teaching specific skills, we are preparing pupils to be life-long readers. Table 1.1 maps the skills from the Key Stage 2 reading curriculum against the content domains to ensure coverage while demonstrating progression as pupils move into Key Stage 3.

Table 1.1   Mapping of KS2 reading curriculum against content domains and KS3 subject content

	Content domain KS2	Skills - national curriculum upper KS2	Subject content - national curriculum KS3
2a	Give/explain the meaning of words in context	Vocabulary development	Understand increasingly challenging texts through: learning new vocabulary, relating it explicitly to known vocabulary and understanding it.
2b	Retrieve and record information/identify key details from fiction and non-fiction	Observation, summarise, decode, skim, scan	Refer to evidence in the text.
2c	Summarise main ideas from more than one paragraph	Make links, summarise, justify	Know the purpose, audience for and context of the writing. Read critically through making critical comparisons across texts.
2d	Make inferences from the text/ explain and justify inferences with evidence from the text	Infer, deduce, empathise, justify, reason, explain, adjust, provide evidence	Understanding increasingly challenging texts through making inferences and referring to evidence in the text.
2e	Predict what might happen from details stated and implied	Predict, infer, evaluate, analyse	Understanding increasingly challenging texts through making inferences and referring to evidence in the text.
2f	Identify/explain how information/narrative content is related and contributes to meaning as a whole	Explain, make links, conceptualise, vocabulary use, infer, evaluate, synthesise	Read critically through studying setting, plot and characterisation, and the effects of these.

	Content domain KS2	Skills – national curriculum upper KS2	Subject content – national curriculum KS3
2g	Identify/explain how meaning is enhanced through choice of words and phrases	Visualise, vocabulary knowledge, knowledge of literary devices, reason, justify	Read critically through knowing how language, including figurative language, vocabulary choice, grammar, text structure and organisational features, presents meaning
2h	Make comparisons within the text	Evaluate, analyse, synthesise, compare, justify	Read critically through making critical comparisons across texts.

Although there is no expectation that pupils dip into the KS3 subject content, it is perhaps useful to have an overview as to expectations, particularly when considering how to develop higher order skills in reading.

Time

Allowing pupils time to read more complex texts, together with providing opportunities to engage in rich discussions, has a time implication. If we consider the requirements of a busy Year 6 classroom and the demands of the curriculum, finding time to ensure pupils engage with texts is difficult. Sharing texts through whole-class reading sessions may provide one solution although this must be followed up by small group reading conferences as explored in Chapter 6. There is little to be gained from children listening to a whole-class text if it is not supplemented by reading discussions which allow pupils to develop the skills that we have outlined in this book. Questioning, providing opinions, justifying answers and building upon existing knowledge are all important components of developing higher-level comprehension skills. The use of peer support groups or reciprocal reading circles or the deployment of additional staff may also go some way to creating time and space to explore challenging texts. There are no quick fixes or easy answers; however, the classroom ethos that is cultivated as part of a reading environment may encourage readers to continue their exploration of texts at home and, as we know from recent research, children who read outside of the classroom are more likely to read above the average reading level for their age (Clark and Teravainen, 2017).

CHAPTER SUMMARY

This chapter has introduced the concept of developing higher-level comprehension skills using challenging texts. Through the exploration of theoretical models which underpin the teaching of reading, you will have a greater understanding of how to teach elements of reading comprehension to best support the development of critical thinking. This chapter serves to position the authors' beliefs and values around what constitutes an advanced reader while providing some examples of what this might look like in practice. By having a more explicit overview of the links between the content domains and the Key Stage 2 and 3 curriculum, you will be able to reflect upon how this may impact upon your own professional practice when supporting and challenging those readers at greater depth.

Further reading

Goouch, K and Lambirth, A (2011) *Teaching Early Reading and Phonics: Creative approaches to early literacy*. London: Sage.

This book provides a comprehensive overview of teaching reading within a broad and balanced curriculum while exploring the research that informs best practice.

www.schoolreadinglist.co.uk/

This is a useful website for providing lists of books suitable for particular age ranges. There is a balance of old and new texts which would enrich any classroom.

References

Almond, D (1998) *Skellig*. London: Hodder Children's Books.

Ballantyne, RM (1982) *The Coral Island*. London: Puffin Books.

Beck, IL, McKeown, MG and Kucan, L (2013) *Bringing Words to Life: Robust vocabulary instruction* (2nd edn). New York: Guilford Press.

Brighton, CM, Moon, TR and Huang, FHL (2015) Advanced readers in reading first classrooms: Who was really 'left behind'? Considerations for the field of gifted education. *Journal for the Education of the Gifted, 38* (3): 257–93.

Chambers, A (2011) *Tell Me: Children reading and talking*. Stroud: Thimble Press.

Clark, C and Teravainen, A (2017) *Celebrating Reading for Enjoyment: Findings from our annual literacy survey 2016*. London: National Literacy Trust.

Clarke, PJ, Snowling, MJ, Truelove, E and Hulme, C (2010) Ameloriating children's reading comprehension difficulties: A randomized control trial, *Psychological Science, 20*: 1–11.

Cremin, T, Mottram, M, Collins, FM, Powell, S and Saford, K (2014) *Building Communities of Engaged Readers: Reading for pleasure*. London: Routledge.

Department for Education (DfE) (2013) *The National Curriculum in England: Framework for Key Stages 1 to 4*. London: DfE.

Elphinstone, A (2018) *Sky Song*. London: Simon & Schuster.

Fang, Z and Pace, BG (2013) Teaching with challenging texts in the disciplines: Text complexity and close reading. *Journal of Adolescent and Adult Literacy, 57* (2): 104–8.

Gee, JP (2004) *Situated Language Learning: A critique of traditional schooling*. Abingdon: Routledge.

Guppy, P and Hughes, M (1999) *The Development of Independent Reading*. Buckingham: Open University Press.

Horton, S, Beattie, L and Bingle, B (2015) *Lessons in Teaching Reading Comprehension in Primary Schools*. London: Sage.

Laird, E (2017) *Welcome to Nowhere*. London: Macmillan Children's Books.

Lambirth, A (2011) Reading, in R Cox (ed.) *Primary English teaching: An introduction to language, literacy and learning*. London: Sage.

McCaughrean, G (2016) *Where the World Ends*. London: Usborne.

Orwell, G (2000 edition) *Animal Farm*. London: Penguin.

Pullman, P (2017) *La Belle Sauvage: The Book of Dust Volume One*. Oxford: Penguin Books.

Reis, SM, Gubbins, EJ, Briggs, C, Schreiber, FJ, Richards, S, Jacobs, J et al. (2004). *Reading Instruction for Talented Readers: Few opportunities for continuous progress.* University of Connecticut, National Research Center on the Gifted and Talented.

Rose, J (2006) *Independent Review of the Teaching of Early Reading*. Nottingham: DfES.

Rundell, K (2017) *The Explorer*. London: Bloomsbury.

Sachar, L (2006) *Small Steps*. London: Bloomsbury.

Shanahan, T, **Fisher, D** and **Frey, N** (2012) The Challenge of Challenging Text. *Educational Leadership, 69* (6): 58–62.

Tolkien, JRR (1955) *Lord of the Rings*. London: George Allen & Unwin.

Wolk, L (2017) *Beyond the Bright Sea*. London: Corgi Children's Books.

2
READING FOR PLEASURE

CHAPTER OBJECTIVES

This chapter will allow you to achieve the following outcomes:

- Have an awareness of the research associated with reading for pleasure;
- Understand some of the challenges associated with higher level reading comprehension;
- Know how to promote reading for pleasure across the school and within your own classroom.

LINKS TO THE TEACHERS' STANDARDS

Working through this chapter will help you meet the following standards:

3. Demonstrate good subject and curriculum knowledge
4. Plan and teach well-structured lessons
5. Adapt teaching to respond to the strengths and needs of all pupils
8. Fulfil wider professional responsibilities

LINKS TO THE NATIONAL CURRICULUM

Pupils should be taught to:

- develop pleasure in reading, motivation to read, vocabulary and understanding by:
  - listening to, discussing and expressing views about a wide range of contemporary and classic poetry, stories and non-fiction at a level beyond that at which they can read independently
  - discussing and clarifying the meanings of words, linking new meanings to known vocabulary
  - discussing their favourite words and phrases

- participate in discussion about books, poems and other works that are read to them and those that they can read for themselves, taking turns and listening to what others say
- explain and discuss their understanding of books, poems and other material, both those that they listen to and those that they read for themselves.

Years 3 and 4 Programme of Study

Reading – comprehension

Pupils should be taught to:

- develop positive attitudes to reading and understanding of what they read by:
  - listening to and discussing a wide range of fiction, poetry, plays, non-fiction and reference books or textbooks
  - reading books that are structured in different ways and reading for a range of purposes.

Years 5 and 6 Programme of Study

Reading – comprehension

Pupils should be taught to:

- maintain positive attitudes to reading and understanding of what they read by:
  - continuing to read and discuss an increasingly wide range of fiction, poetry, plays, non-fiction and reference books or textbooks
  - reading books that are structured in different ways and reading for a range of purposes
  - increasing their familiarity with a wide range of books, including myths, legends and traditional stories, modern fiction, fiction from our literary heritage, and books from other cultures and traditions.

(DfE, 2013)

What is reading for pleasure?

There is little doubt that reading for pleasure is fundamental to developing lifelong readers. Indeed, one of the overarching aims of the national curriculum is that all pupils *develop the habit of reading widely and often, for both pleasure and information* (DfE, 2013, p3). But what does it actually mean? There are many definitions of the term 'reading for pleasure', ranging from the creative nature of the pastime (Holden, 2004) to ones that explore feelings associated with the act of reading (McKenna *et al.*, 2012). However, a definition that seems to resonate with classroom practice comes from the National Literacy Trust, which states that reading for pleasure is *reading that we do of our own free will, anticipating the satisfaction that we will get from the act of reading* (Clark and Rumbold, 2006, p5). If children read because they are truly interested in what lies between the pages, there is an increasing likelihood that they will choose to replicate this behaviour as they move into young adulthood. Therefore it is imperative that the habit of reading for pleasure and enjoyment is nurtured from early childhood. Studies have shown that attainment is higher in children that demonstrate enjoyment in reading (Clark and De Zoysa, 2011; Petscher 2010; Twist *et al.*, 2012), although it is interesting to note that some of our higher achieving readers reported low levels of reading enjoyment (Twist *et al.*, 2012), something that was replicated on a much smaller scale in the case study below. Furthermore, the number of children reading for pleasure seems to be stagnating as evidenced in international surveys such as the PIRLS and PISA studies (Mullis *et al*, 2012; OECD, 2009). A report produced in 2012 by Ofsted, as a consequence of these two international studies, strongly recommended that schools implement whole-school policies to address reading engagement through the development of a clear reading for pleasure strategy (Ofsted, 2012). However, there appears to have been little follow-up work which assessed the impact of this on children's reading habits and little evidence that this has been noted by Ofsted during routine inspections, despite some excellent practice by schools.

CASE STUDY: BUILDING A READING FOR PLEASURE COMMUNITY

This case study explores how a whole-school reading promotion plan led to:

- an increase in pupils choosing to read for pleasure;
- improved attainment in reading;
- a heightened awareness among staff of the importance of modelling reading for pleasure.

The school was participating in an international research project to improve literacy by convincing all stakeholders about the need to devote more time and effort to reading promotion and to place reading for pleasure at the centre of their policies, approaches and practices (Horton *et al.*, 2013). The programme consisted of reading promotion activities from the 'Lifelong Readers' Project web-site (**www.lifelongreaders.org**), trialled in school to evaluate effectiveness and suitability, together with planned whole-school events in order to: raise the profile of reading within the school and wider community; raise standards of attainment in reading; encourage a willingness to read for pleasure and to encourage confident, enthusiastic readers.

During training workshops delivered by the lead researcher, teachers completed a whole-school audit together with a personal profile indicating areas around reading engagement that would benefit from improvement. Pupils were interviewed to gain qualitative data around their perceptions of reading within the school and to gauge their attitudes to reading within a wider context. Initial findings before implementation of the reading promotion plan indicated that:

- Pupils already felt quite confident in their ability to read and enjoyed reading, with the majority of pupils indicating that they strongly agreed or agreed with statements that asked for this information.

- All pupils participating in the study felt that reading was a worthwhile activity and most felt supported by their teachers at school, although agreement with this statement declined slightly for pupils in KS2.
- All pupils could list their favourite books and authors and were able to articulate this; however, this was drawn from a narrow canon of children's literature.
- Some pupils did not feel their teachers liked reading and some pupils stated that they did not see their teachers reading in the classroom on a regular basis.
- Teachers stated that they were confident that all their pupils enjoyed reading although data from pupils indicated that they themselves were not aware of this.

Although statutory assessment scores were above the national average, the school felt that further development of reading for pleasure and the embedding of this into daily practice would benefit all pupils based on analysis of the interim data. The main areas to be addressed were: visibility of reading within school; teachers as readers; suitability and use of the school library; and reading events to promote reading for pleasure.

Teachers implemented a number of reading promotion strategies to raise the visibility of reading within the school. Reading recommendations, reading cafes and teacher/pupil conferences contributed to building communities of readers. Whole-school events including dressing up as a book character, extreme reading and author of the term increased the visibility of reading across the school. Teachers identifying their favourite books and displaying these within the classroom led to pupils acknowledging that their teachers enjoyed reading which contributed to a school-wide reading for pleasure ethos. An overnight event whereby parents were invited to share stories with their children before leaving them to enjoy a sleepover at school helped secure parental engagement as did a monthly newsletter to parents highlighting suitable texts and activities to share at home.

Data was subsequently collated following the implementation of the programme and indications suggested that the reading promotion activities delivered across the school were successful in raising the profile of reading. Results from the research found that:

- More children were reading a wider range of books and authors.
- More children stated that they read in their free time at school and at home.
- More children expressed enjoyment in visiting libraries and book shops.
- Children reported a greater parental involvement in children's reading at school and at home.
- More children indicated that they thought their teachers enjoyed reading.
- Teachers felt more confident in promoting reading for pleasure.

One of the most significant impacts was upon children reading at home and choosing to read during their free time and in the school holidays. In addition, results showed that more pupils were choosing to visit bookshops and libraries (including the school library) indicating an upsurge in the enjoyment of reading. Furthermore, statutory tests taken in Year 2 demonstrated even higher levels of attainment in reading.

(Continued)

(Continued)

Case study reflections

- How do you ensure that you are seen as a reader within the context of the classroom?
- In what ways do you involve pupils in the design of reading promotion activities so as to build upon their interests?
- What might pupils say about your attitude to reading and does this represent a true reflection of your values?

The importance of reading for pleasure

Studies have found that reading for pleasure is closely linked to educational achievement and has a greater impact upon attainment than socio-economic factors or parents' level of education (OECD, 2002; Sullivan and Brown, 2013). There is also long-standing evidence which suggests that reading for pleasure impacts positively upon general knowledge and improves children's general social skills (Cunningham and Stanovich, 1998; Allan *et al.*, 2005; Reading Agency, 2006). A more recent literature review by the Reading Agency cites evidence from a number of studies which state that reading for pleasure improves social relationships and interactions, develops empathy and can enhance communication skills (Reading Agency, 2015). This provides a compelling argument for placing reading for pleasure firmly at the heart of the English curriculum.

RESEARCH FOCUS: BUILDING COMMUNITIES OF READERS

This United Kingdom Literacy Association (UKLA) project conducted by Cremin *et al.* was in direct response to evidence that suggested children in England were less likely to read for pleasure than children in other countries (Twist, 2007). Previous research by the UKLA found that of the 1,200 primary teachers questioned, the majority were relying on a limited canon of children's literature to use in the classroom.

It is debatable ... whether teachers are familiar with a wide enough range of children's authors in order to plan richly integrated and holistic literacy work.

(Cremin *et al.*, 2008, p458)

Therefore, the project had the following aims:

- to widen teachers' knowledge of children's literature;
- to develop teachers' confidence and skilful use of such literature in the classroom;
- to develop teachers' relationships with parents, carers, librarians and families;
- to develop 'Reading Teachers', teachers who read and readers who teach.

Developing reading for pleasure in the classroom

Despite statistics from the National Literacy Trust's annual survey demonstrating that pupils at Key Stage 4 are enjoying reading more than in previous years, there is still a significant gap between the percentage of pupils stating that they enjoy reading at Key Stage 4 when compared with Key Stage 2 (43.4 per cent compared with 65.6 per cent). Not only do Key Stage 2 children enjoy reading more, they also read more frequently outside of the classroom than children in Key Stage 3 and 4 (Clark, 2015). There is also a body of evidence that suggests that, as children grow older, they are less likely to read for pleasure (Topping, 2010; Clark and Douglas, 2011). Therefore, it is imperative that this is addressed with pupils as they reach upper Key Stage 2 in order to avoid falling into the downward spiral of non-engagement with reading as is often experienced at secondary school. How can we ensure that our pupils continue to be interested and motivated to read and that we are effectively challenging our higher-level readers while supporting individual learners to make progress? There are three key areas which contribute to promoting positive attitudes towards reading:

- ethos

- environment

- engagement.

Ethos

The importance of establishing a reading for pleasure ethos should not be underestimated. Making time for pupils to choose and share books with teachers and their peers will contribute towards building a community of readers within the classroom. Valuing pupils' views on what they have read is pivotal when looking to foster a love of reading as it allows children to engage in purposeful conversations. A useful tool to introduce this in the classroom is Aidan Chambers' 'book talk' (Chambers, 2011) where the teacher guides group discussions by carefully selecting questions which will provoke thought and promote discussion. This allows children to engage with the text on a much deeper level as they share ideas and co-construct meaning within a mutually supportive framework (Horton *et al.*, 2014). Exploring their thoughts and reactions to a variety of texts will only serve to enhance the importance of reading within the classroom and for this to take place we must ensure that time is set aside on a daily basis to facilitate matters.

CASE STUDY: USING BOOK TALK IN THE CLASSROOM

Rebecca's school had a whole-school policy of independent reading for 15 minutes at the start of every afternoon and her Year 5 class would randomly select books from the reading corner and return them within a few minutes, replacing them for a different text. Rebecca felt that many of her pupils were not making informed choices but were grabbing books from the shelf as there was

(Continued)

(Continued)

an expectation that they needed to read silently for 15 minutes. She decided to explore this further with her class and it became apparent that they found it difficult to select appropriate texts. Choice was fairly limited and most of the books had seen better days! Many of the children in her class could not find a book that would interest them, and the less confident readers were unable to browse in order to make an appropriate choice. She realised that she needed to model this process so that children were able to successfully make choices and that she needed to build a library of books that pupils in her class would want to choose.

Rebecca asked her pupils to bring in a favourite book from their home collection so that they could share with peers. She instigated the '30-second convincer' activity whereby one pupil had 30 seconds to convince their group why they should read a particular book. Rebecca modelled the process, articulating her thought processes so that the pupils in her class were able to replicate this. This led to a wider range of texts in the classroom and a greater buzz around reading. It also meant that pupils had the opportunity to discuss texts and voice their opinions as to whether or not they had enjoyed reading a particular item.

Rebecca soon realised the benefits of her pupils chatting about what they had read and set up smaller reading groups in which pupils could discuss a book that they had all read. Question prompts were provided to promote discussion and to ensure pupils were developing higher order thinking skills. Examples of questions were drawn from Aidan Chambers' 'Tell Me' framework (Chambers, 2011) and included:

- What did you like/dislike about the book? Why?
- Were there any surprises in the book?
- Did anything puzzle you?
- Did this book remind you of anything?
- Why do you think the main character acted in this way?
- Would you have done the same thing? Why? Why not?
- Who was your favourite character? Why?

These 15-minute reading sessions soon became something that the children looked forward to and the idea quickly spread to the rest of the school. Engaging children in meaningful discussions about books raised the profile of reading within the classroom and provided the teacher with opportunities to assess understanding. The use of question prompts to encourage children to explain how and why they had come to their conclusions about the text was key in identifying next steps for individual learners.

Case study reflections

- How do you ensure that your classroom ethos supports reading for pleasure?
- How are you using key questions to develop understanding and build on comprehension skills?
- What do you consider to be the benefits of reading groups?

The importance of building supportive communities of readers is essential if we are to encourage pupils to read willingly and freely. Research by Cremin *et al.* suggested that teachers should develop readers through *encouraging interaction, choice, autonomy and increased reading for pleasure* (Cremin *et al.*, 2009, p3). The role of the teacher in nurturing readers can have, as we have seen from the case studies above, a significant influence on attitudes.

Environment

As you walk through school, what messages are conveyed around reading and the value that is placed on it? Author of the month display boards and reading recommendation walls will allow children opportunities to widen their reading repertoire. Reading areas in classrooms provide comfortable and stimulating environments in which children can explore a variety of genres. Shared reading spaces allow children a place in which to engage in discussion about their book of choice. By providing children with access to an attractive reading area which contains a wide variety of reading material, you will be promoting reading which will ultimately lead to increased enjoyment. As we know from the research cited earlier, positive attitudes to reading result in an increase in attainment (Clark and Rumbold, 2006). When considering children's interests, it may be beneficial to include e-books and tablets as part of your reading material as well as book-based texts to ensure a truly inclusive reading environment. A well-designed reading area which actively seeks to promote both independent and collaborative reading opportunities is essential when considering the reading environment (Reutzel and Fawson, 2004; Lockwood, 2008).

By providing access to a reading area that contains diverse reading material, you will be promoting reading which in itself will lead to increased engagement, thus contributing to increased attainment. An effectively designed book area which provides opportunities for children to engage in independent and collaborative reading is crucial when developing reading environments (Reutzel and Fawson, 2004; Lockwood, 2008). There are a number of ways in which you can create an inviting reading environment:

- Consider the furniture. Is it comfortable? Does it lend itself to quiet reading time? Are there areas to sit together?

- Have you included e-books and tablets to ensure an inclusive reading environment?

- Do the shelves reflect children's reading interests?

- Is there a range of reading material – comics, magazines, non-fiction texts, leaflets, catalogues, instruction manuals, graphic novels, poetry books, audio books?

- How often do children access their reading area? Is it an integral part of the classroom?

- Use posters such as the National Literacy Trust's Premier League Reading Stars to inspire young readers (**https://literacytrust.org.uk/programmes/sport-and-literacy/premier-league-primary-stars/**)

Engagement

Reading is a multi-faceted construct which relies on an arsenal of strategies to achieve success and one may be forgiven for prioritising the skills of reading over what Cremin describes as the 'the will' due to the statutory requirements of the national curriculum which places word recognition at the forefront of teaching children to read. However, there is no denying the fact that 'the will' is pivotal in securing the best possible outcomes for pupils (Cremin *et al.*, 2014). Research evidence provides a strong correlation between reading for pleasure and increased attainment (OECD, 2002; Clark and de Zoysa, 2011) which suggests that these two areas are not mutually exclusive. The most successful classrooms are those where teachers are skilled in reading pedagogies and have a holistic view of the reading process.

Engaging with reading outside of the classroom is another key element in increasing attainment in reading. A report published by the National Literacy Trust reported that children who read outside of the classroom on a regular basis were much more likely to be reading at a level above age related expectations (Clark and Poulton, 2011). Once again, evidence from international studies focuses on regular reading outside of school and the difference that this can make to reading assessment scores (PIRLS, 2006; OECD, 2010). Links between home and school are essential if we are to truly foster positive attitudes to reading and develop children, not only as competent readers, but also as life-long readers. Dialogue between home and school is crucial, whether through reading diaries or logs which warrant comments from children and parents. However, it is essential that sharing reading books does not become a chore or simply a tick box exercise. Interaction between parents and children is crucial and as Michael Lockwood is keen to point out:

> *The best way parents can help the teacher, usually, is by encouraging pleasure reading at home, by reading together with their children and talking about books read, rather than through trying to teach reading.*
>
> (Lockwood, 2008, p39)

Successful schools aim to increase parental engagement to secure best possible outcomes for pupils and to build a wider community of readers. They devote time to working alongside parents to secure positive reading habits for their children.

CASE STUDY

This primary school values reading for pleasure and is committed to engaging parents in sharing books and developing reading at home. Reading meetings begin in Reception, with parents being invited to attend a short meeting and a series of workshops where children share their own thoughts and views on reading. These are repeated as children move into different year groups, and each has a different focus. In Reception, parents are provided with guidance on how to share books and explore illustrations and picture books so that parent and child can have those rich conversations around narrative, character and setting as suggested in Chapter 3. The meeting in Year 2 focuses on developing comprehension skills and questioning techniques, with suggested reading lists on offer. As pupils move into Key Stage 2, the focus becomes more targeted: activities such as 'Dad's reading' and reading challenges (including the National Literacy Trust's football challenge **www.literacytrust.org.uk/premier_league_reading_stars**) are central to home/school reading liaison, while Year 6 meetings centre on higher order skills and providing a challenge for more able readers, together with recommendations for appropriate reading material. In addition, parents have opportunities to attend guided reading sessions in school so as to enhance their understanding of how reading is developed in school through observing teachers modelling reading for purpose and pleasure.

The school also provides many other activities and opportunities. For example:

- book quizzes for children and parents;
- book fairs;
- extreme reading competitions;
- bedtime reading sessions (parents are invited into school to share a story with their child over a hot chocolate);
- reading clubs;
- attendance at class assemblies where reading for pleasure is a central theme;
- reading challenges;
- competitions;
- visits from authors.

(Horton *et al.*, 2015)

Case study reflections

- How have you developed a reading community that stretches beyond the school walls?
- In what ways do you engage parents, particularly in Key Stage 2?

The case study above illustrates how you can encourage parents to become more involved in their child's reading and foster positive reading habits. Needless to say, attainment in reading was very high across the school.

Using challenging texts within the classroom

How do we define challenging texts? Often, when looking for texts to challenge readers, readability is a key factor with complexity of words and sentence length dictating choice. There are a number of readability formulae used to determine readability scores which focus on how understanding of the words and sentences affects comprehension (Tennent, 2015). However, when considering the use of challenging texts in the classroom, consider the bigger picture: vocabulary, coherence, organisation of the text and prior knowledge.

Providing challenging texts in the classroom allows children the opportunity to deepen their understanding and sharpen their comprehension skills. It also stimulates imagination, motivates the reader and encourages emotional connections with character; however, there is evidence to suggest that both boys and girls tend to choose books that are easier to read once they reach

Year 6 (Topping, 2010). When we think of challenging texts, books such as Tolkien's *Lord of the Rings, A Christmas Carol* by Dickens or any of Shakespeare's plays may spring to mind. However, picture books such as Anthony Browne's *Voices in the Park* or *Duck, Death and the Tulip* by Wolf Erlbruch can provide challenge for readers through the demands they make on the reader to look more deeply into the text. Books such as *Scarlet Ibis* by Gill Lewis and *The Naming of Tishkin Silk* by Glenda Millard tackle hard-hitting themes such as the loss of a sibling and mental health and can be considered challenging texts in their own right. Skilful use of questioning, discussion and talk is needed to ensure children have the opportunity to re-shape their ideas and articulate their thoughts. Not only will this improve comprehension skills, it will also broaden children's reading choices and may lead to children encountering a more diverse range of reading material. However, there are challenges associated with the use of such texts in the classroom and we must be mindful of this when choosing and sharing texts with the class.

Themes

Make sure that you have read the book yourself before sharing it with the class. It is important to model how challenging texts can be enjoyable, stimulating and emotional through your own reactions to texts but be aware of how this may affect individuals. A few years ago, I was working alongside a class teacher who was reading *Journey to Jo'Burg* by Beverley Naidoo to her Year 5 class when she became so overcome with emotion that she was unable to continue. Reading Lord Tennyson's *The Lady of Shalott* one day to a group of Year 6 children, I remember looking down to see two children with silent tears running down their cheeks and it was at that moment that I realised they had truly connected with the poem and had invested a great deal of emotion into that lesson. Know your texts and know your children.

Decoding v comprehension

Some texts are challenging because of the language used and can be problematic in terms of word recognition. Shakespeare's plays or Chaucer's tales (although choose wisely!) are rich with language but may need a little more attention paid when approaching unfamiliar words. Reading books which contain unfamiliar language can also develop fluency as pupils will need to re-read extracts in order to make sense of the text. Consider how you want to challenge readers in your class while promoting reading for pleasure. If a text is too difficult, individuals may shy away from similar texts but if you are using texts to explore meaning, there are many options. There are a number of children's versions of Shakespeare's plays which do not replicate the original language; however, these texts explore themes and offer opportunities for discussion. I know of many a child that has developed a love of Shakespeare in this way while being prepared for study at Key Stage 3 and 4.

Time

Some of the more challenging texts that children wish to engage with can be lengthy tomes: take, for example, *Tom's Midnight Garden* by Philippa Pearce or *Harry Potter and the Order of the Phoenix* by JK Rowling, not forgetting the *Percy Jackson* series by Rick Riordan. These can take time to read so strategies to encourage stamina are necessary to ensure engagement. Reading groups are ideal to address this, as pupils will be reading independently but meeting together to discuss the book, therefore there is an expectation that the text is read outside of the classroom.

Ensuring breadth

There are many factors that contribute to the complexity of a text: themes, sentence construction, language, vocabulary, coherence and length. In order for children to benefit from a breadth of reading experiences, they need to have these presented to them on a regular basis. We can all recall an advanced reader who persistently chose books from the same series and while this is important to nurture, we, as teachers, need to gently coax individuals out of their comfort zone and encourage them to challenge themselves. Peer and teacher recommendations are key to exposing pupils to books which they may not necessarily choose for themselves. If we think back to developing a reading ethos in the classroom, allowing children time to talk to others about what they are reading will create a more diverse list from which to choose.

CHAPTER SUMMARY

Within this chapter, we have explored some of the associated pedagogies around reading for pleasure and enjoyment. It is crucial that teachers have a comprehensive knowledge of children's literature in order to encourage choice and there are many online lists of recommended books available, of which some are included in the recommended reading below. Reading environments, opportunities for discussion, reading communities and book recommendations all contribute to developing a reading for pleasure culture within school. This chapter links theory to practice by drawing upon significant research and marrying this with practical approaches explored in the case studies. Schools, teachers and parents and carers have a fundamental role to play in promoting reading for pleasure and this chapter has explored some of the strategies that will support pupils to develop as lifelong readers.

References

Allan, J, Ellis, S and **Pearson, C** (2005) *Literature Circles, Gender and Reading for Enjoyment*. Edinburgh: Scottish Executive.

Browne, A (1999) *Voices in the Park*. London: Random House.

Chambers, A (2011) *Tell Me: Children reading and talk*. Stroud: Thimble Press.

Clark, C (2015) *Children's and young people's reading in 2014: Findings from the 2014 National Literacy Trust's annual survey*. London: National Literacy Trust.

Clark, C and de Zoysa, S (2011) *Mapping the interrelationships of reading enjoyment, attitudes, behaviour and attainment: An exploratory investigation*. London: National Literacy Trust.

Clark, C and Douglas, J (2011) *Young people's reading and writing: An in depth study focusing on enjoyment, behaviour, attitudes and attainment*. London: National Literacy Trust.

Clark, C and Poulton, L (2011) *Book ownership and its relation to reading enjoyment, attitudes, behaviour and attainment.* London: National Literacy Trust.

Clark, C and Rumbold, K (2006) *Reading for pleasure: A research overview.* London: National Literacy Trust.

Cremin, T, Mottram, M, Bearne, E and Goodwin, P (2008) Exploring teachers' knowledge of children's literature, *Cambridge Journal of Education, 38* (4): 449–64.

Cremin, T, Mottram, M, Collins, F , Powell, S and Safford, K (2009) Teachers as readers: building communities of readers, *Literacy, 43* (1): pp. 11–19.

Cremin, T, Mottram, M, Powell, S, Collins, R and Safford, K (2014) *Building Communities of Engaged Readers: Reading for pleasure.* London: Routledge.

Cunningham, AE and Stanovich, KE (1998) What reading does for the mind. *American Educator, 22* (1 and 2): 8–15.

Department for Education (DfE) (2013) *The National Curriculum in England: Framework for Key Stages 1 to 4.* London: DfE.

Dickens, C (2003) *A Christmas Carol.* London: Puffin Classics.

Erlbruch, W (2008) *Duck, Death and the Tulip.* Wellington: Gecko Press.

Holden, J (2004) *Creative Reading.* London: Demos.

Horton, S, Beattie, L and Bingle, B (2015) *Lessons in Teaching Reading Comprehension in Primary School.* London: Sage/Learning Matters.

Horton, S, Sullivan, P and Robertson, C (2013) *Lifelong readers: A European reading promotion framework for primary school librarians, educators and administrators (LiRe). A report based on findings from England and Ireland.* Cyprus: CARDET.

Horton, S *et al*. (2014) *Lessons in Teaching Grammar in Primary Schools.* London: Learning Matters/ Sage.

Lewis, G (2014) *Scarlet Ibis.* Oxford: Oxford University Press.

Lockwood, M (2008) *Promoting Reading for Pleasure in the Primary School.* London: Sage.

McKenna, MC, Conradi, K, Lawrence, C, Jang, BG and **Meyer, JP** (2012) Reading attitudes of middle school students: Results of a U.S. survey. *Reading Research Quarterly, 47* (3): 283–306.

Millard, G (2013) *The naming of Tishkin Silk.* London: Phoenix Yard Books.

Mullis, IVS, Martin, MO, Foy, P and Drucker, KT (2012) *PIRLS 2011 international results in reading.* Chestnut Hill, MA: Boston College.

Naidoo, B (1987) *Journey to Jo'Burg.* London: Collins.

Ofsted (2012) *Moving English Forward.* London: Ofsted.

Organisation for Economic Co-operation and Development (OECD) (2002) *Reading for change: Results from PISA 2000.* **www.oecd.org/education/school/programmeforinternationalstudentassessmentpisa/33690986.pdf**.

Organisation for Economic Co-operation and Development (OECD) (2009) *PISA 2009 results: Executive summary.* OECD.

Pearce, P (2015) *Tom's Midnight Garden.* Oxford. OUP (reissue edition).

Petscher, Y (2010) A meta-analysis of the relationship between student attitudes towards reading and achievement in reading. *Journal of Research in Reading, 33* (4): 335–55.

PIRLS (2006) *Assessment.* International Association for the Evaluation of Educational Achievement (IEA), TIMSS & PIRLS International Study Center, Lynch School of Education, Boston College.

Reading Agency (2006) *The Summer Reading Challenge 2005.* London: TRA.

Reading Agency (2015) *Literature Review: The impact of reading for pleasure and empowerment*, BOP Consulting. Available: **https://readingagency.org.uk/news/The%20Impact%20of%20 Reading%20for%20Pleasure%20and%20Empowerment.pdf**

Reutzel DR and Fawson PC (2004) *Your Classroom Library: New ways to give it more teaching power.* London: Scholastic.

Rowling, JK (2007) *Harry Potter and the Order of the Phoenix.* London: Bloomsbury.

Sullivan, A and Brown, M (2013) *Social inequalities in cognitive scores at age 16: The role of reading*, CLS Working Paper 2013/10. London: Centre for Longitudinal Studies. **www.cls.ioe.ac.uk/ shared/getfile.ashx?itemtype=document&id=1719**

Tennent, W (2015) *Understanding Reading Comprehension: Processes and practices.* London: Sage.

Tennyson, A (2013) *The Lady of Shalott.* Oxford: Oxford University Press.

TIMSS & PIRLS International Study Center [online]. Available: **https://timssandpirls. bc.edu/pirls2011/reports/international-results-pirls.html** (last accessed 20 November 2017).

Tolkien, JRR (2005) *The Lord of the Rings.* London: HarperCollins.

Topping, KJ (2010). *What Kids are Reading: The book-reading habits of students in British schools, 2010.* London: Renaissance Learning UK.

Twist, L, Schagen, I, and Hodgson, C (2007) *Readers and Reading: the PIRLS 2006 National Report for England.* Slough: NFER.

Twist, L, Sizmur, J, Bartlett, S and Lynn, L (2012) *PIRLS 2011: Reading Achievement in England.* Slough: NFER

3
VARIETY OF TEXTS

- ○ reading books that are structured in different ways and reading for a range of purposes
- ○ increasing their familiarity with a wide range of books, including myths, legends and traditional stories, modern fiction, fiction from our literary heritage, and books from other cultures and traditions
- ○ recommending books that they have read to their peers, giving reasons for their choices
- ○ identifying and discussing themes and conventions in and across a wide range of writing
- ○ making comparisons within and across books
- ○ learning a wider range of poetry by heart
- ○ preparing poems and plays to read aloud and to perform, showing understanding through intonation, tone and volume so that the meaning is clear to an audience

(DfE, 2013)

The importance of using a variety of texts

All reading begins with selection.

(Chambers, 2011, p16)

You have already seen in Chapter 2 how reading for pleasure is instrumental not only in inspiring readers, but also in developing knowledge, creativity and confidence. Reading can unlock children's full potential and those children that can read well have access to an infinite range of experiences that 'real life' may not offer. Without a doubt, this can support progress in school. Children who are engaged in reading learn more from their classroom lessons; as they read more, they become better readers who can recognise words and make sense of them, leading to greater learning in other subjects (Dombey, 2010). Further research confirms that children who enjoy reading are working 'at' or 'better than' age-expected criteria, while those who do not enjoy reading are often working 'below' (Clark and Rumbold, 2006). Therefore, whether your focus is to inspire your children to be confident, enthusiastic, developed readers or to guide them to be better scholars (hopefully, both!), if they do not have access to a range of quality texts, neither is likely.

In the absence of interesting texts, very little is possible.

(Williams, 1986, p42)

Williams' emphatic statement is echoed by Chambers (2011) who suggests that the selection of a book, hearing it read aloud and having the opportunity to talk about it are the three main factors in developing readers (Chambers 2011). If children are to become independent, fluent readers who can choose a book and enjoy it (Cremin *et al.*, 2014), then children need a variety of texts to choose from in the first place. The national curriculum (DfE, 2013) states that this should include: poetry, plays, non-fiction and reference books, textbooks, myths, legends and traditional stories, modern fiction, fiction from our literary heritage, and books from other cultures and traditions. That is quite a library! If children have only a few texts to choose from, or if the books that are available are not the kind of books that appeal to them, then the chances of children finding one they *want* to read is small (Chambers 2011). If you also add to the equation that the selection should include *books and authors that they might not choose to read themselves* (DfE, 2013) then a variety of texts, and knowledge around the texts, is essential.

Choosing challenging texts – developing your reader

How do you define a challenging text?

Gallagher (2004) compares reading to a baseball game – even the most uninterested spectator can understand it on a surface level, but it takes further engagement, practice and study to enjoy the complexities and nuances of the game that help to understand it on a deeper level. This, she states, is like reading; you need to be taught how to *dig below the surface of text and read nuances of the game* (Gallagher, 2004, p4). This is the fundamental key to a challenging text – is there scope for the reader to 'dig deeper', developing those essential comprehension skills? What exactly should the reader be doing and how can the text choice, and indeed the teacher, be supporting this?

What are the features of a challenging text?

Hoffman *et al.* (2015) emphasise that the *what* to read is just as important as the *how* to read, with some children's books providing more to think about than others. They consider that in terms of challenging books, teachers' book choices should be focused on those that offer multi-layered interpretations. Through collaboration and exploratory talk, there should be opportunities for children to co-construct meaning and personal interpretation of the text (Horton *et al.*, 2015).

For a book to be considered 'complex', consideration should be given to those that are thematically rich, contain 'rounded' characters which are multi-dimensional, comprise complex and engaging illustrations (where used) and have rich language and a complex plot.

Shanahan *et al.* (2012) agree, elaborating that, in addition, vocabulary is important and that there should be a balance between the element of challenge posed by the vocabulary within a text with the amount of known vocabulary needed to access the text. They also state that the complexity of the sentence structure by writers can often be so multi-layered that children also need the opportunity to make sense of the conventions of text, e.g. multiple phrases, clauses and punctuation. Therefore, when considering a challenging text, teachers should determine whether these features apply.

How do you choose a challenging text?

Of course, in any Key Stage 2 class, the children's ability to dig deeper will be on many different levels, depending on their engagement with the text and their ability to read the lines, read between the lines and read beyond the lines (Horton *et al.*, 2015), emphasising the ongoing need for the class teacher to know their pupils. However, the following questions may help to ascertain the level of challenge in the text:

- Is there opportunity for the reader to apply their own interpretations to the text?

- Are the themes or author's voice challenging the reader to consider areas they may be unfamiliar with?

- Is the vocabulary accessible, yet challenging for the reader, offering imagery they can explore?

- Is the sentence structure complex enough to challenge the reader at times?

- Is the narrative structure or cohesion between paragraphs particularly thought-provoking?

To accommodate this, teachers need to know and understand their children and have access to an appropriate and wide range of books to scaffold these 'layers' of understanding. It would be worth noting, however, that there is no expectation for a book to contain *all* these factors to be determined as 'challenging'. For example, David Almond's contemporary and popular *Skellig* is a clear example of a modern fiction text which has a wonderful ambiguity. On a simple level, it is a beautiful story of a young boy, Michael, who finds comfort in helping the strange character he finds in his garage, a much-needed escape from the upset surrounding him as his family cope with Michael's desperately ill new-born baby sister and a chaotic house-move. The sentence structure, vocabulary and short chapters mean the text is largely accessible. However, there are many layers to the book, allowing the emphasis to be on the depth of the themes and the parallels between Skellig's recovery and that of his sister. There is also allegory, the author's attitudes to social care and relationships between adults and children, all of which can provide more challenge for a reader. This supports the notion in Chapter 2 that providing a challenging text allows children the opportunity to deepen their understanding and improve their comprehension skills.

Commentary: *Footpath Flowers* by Jon Arno Lawson and Sydney Smith

This beautiful, wordless picture book could be explored by a reader of any age who would enjoy the poignant illustrations depicting a young girl walking home with her father. While the girl finds pleasure in the little things around her, her father impatiently continues the journey, mainly on his mobile phone, stopping only for the girl to catch up. She, on the other hand, collects flowers growing in unlikely places among the cracks of the urban landscape and gifts them to unexpected recipients. A simple story with no words – could this be a challenging text? Using the features of a challenging text (above), this book is certainly thematically rich, the characters are multi-dimensional and the illustrations offer many layers of interpretation. The use of picture books to develop inference has been well documented (O'Neill, 2011; Horton *et al.*, 2015) and through careful questioning, *Footpath Flowers* could be used to explore the reader's perceptions of giving; relationships between parents and their children; journeys (both physical and emotional) and a child's perspective on society. Readers could explore the use of colour – how is it used? Why does the colour develop? Does this reflect the author's voice? What impact does it have on the reader? How do the visual aspects of the book contribute to the 'feel' of it? The impact of the girl's actions could be explored, both in terms of the points in the book (giving flowers to a sleeping man) and linked to a wider scale in society (exploring the issues that could lead to the man sleeping on a bench). Why has Smith chosen to use smaller boxes and whole-page illustrations? What is the significance? What is the impact? There is a multitude of layers of analysis and evaluation in *Footpath Flowers* which can be explored at a more complex level, therefore it can be acknowledged as a challenging text.

Challenges of variety of texts

So how do teachers ensure they have a selection of books which not only match the requirements of the national curriculum, including books and authors that children may not have met themselves, but also match the needs of their children? While enthusing them and challenging them? What are the challenges of knowing which texts to use with which pupils?

CASE STUDY: ONE TEACHER'S JOURNEY TO IMPROVING HER KNOWLEDGE OF A VARIETY OF CHILDREN'S BOOKS

This case study explores one teacher's journey to improve her knowledge of children's texts. Jacqui had always used a text as a focus for her literacy lessons with her Year 6 class. For the past few years she had used *Stormbreaker* (Horowitz, 2015) in the autumn term and *Private Peaceful* (Morpurgo, 2004) in the summer term. Both were books which she had originally chosen as not only would they appeal to boys due to their genre and themes but they met the needs of the national curriculum in terms of *a wide range of fiction, including modern fiction* (DfE, 2013, p43). The school had invested in a class set of each and she had developed a bank of resources for both to which she added each year. Jacqui knew the books well and had annotated her own copy with questions and prompts. The children also had access to a very well-resourced school library where they would choose their own reading books. Jacqui was happy that children were supported to *maintain positive attitudes to reading and an understanding of what they read* (DfE, 2013, p43).

However, during a staff meeting where colleagues were asked to request new books for the library, she realised that she had a 'go-to' list of authors including Michael Morpurgo, Roald Dahl and Jacqueline Wilson, and some classics from her own time at school, but little beyond that. Looking at her class's reading books, children were reading *Diary of a Wimpy Kid*, David Walliams novels and *Tom Gates*. She realised that if she wanted her class to engage in a wide range of reading and have the opportunity for a deep understanding of texts, then she would need to introduce them to a much wider range of authors and texts. But where to start?

Jacqui joined a reading teachers group which met half-termly; the aim of the group was for the 'Reader Leader' to choose a book which was to be revealed at the meeting. Each teacher was to then buy their own copy with the view to reading it, sharing it in some way with their class and discussing it at the next meeting. Jacqui was surprised when the first book was introduced; it was wrapped in old-looking brown paper with key words written across it: time-travel, magic, war, survival, eternity, friends and enemies. Even among a group of teachers everyone was excited – what could this book inside be? Jacqui had never heard of *The 1,000-Year-Old Boy* by Ross Welford and admitted it would not normally be her usual choice of book, but by already having a clue to some of the themes and motifs inside the book, she felt inspired.

Jacqui had already shared with her class the fact that she was attending a book group that evening and had been surprised at how interested the class were. She re-wrapped her book, then repeated the same thing with the class the next day – there was a surge of excitement.

Consequently, she used her book to read to the class for ten minutes at the end of the day and whenever they had time, which wasn't easy in a pressured curriculum, but the children were excited to read alongside their teacher. As a result, two of her avid readers bought their own copy and another student asked for any Ross Welford books for her birthday. As it wasn't a 'study book' for the class, Jacqui did not feel pressure to plan sessions around the book, but instead used talk to naturally enthuse and elicit responses from the children. Children began to make comparisons with the themes in *Stormbreaker* (and later with *Private Peaceful*) and there was a genuine interest in the author too. Conversations evolved: what other books did they know with similar themes? If they were buying this on Amazon, what books would pop up as being 'similar'? Sum up the book in one sentence.

By the end of the school year, Jacqui had six new books that she would never have come across before which she shared with the children and kept in the classroom for the children to use. More importantly, it had shown her class that she was a reader too, with opinions, likes and dislikes. It had inspired her to step outside of her comfort zone and explore new books which could then be shared outside of 'set texts'. (The Cheltenham Festival Reading Teachers = Reading Pupils offer a similar group.)

Case study reflections

- How do you keep abreast of new/relevant books?
- How do you select quality texts to use in the classroom?
- How do you share your texts and inspire your children?

Jacqui's story reflects that of many teachers. Cremin *et al.* (2009) suggests that in their personal lives, many teachers are avid readers, but professionally they rely on a very limited circle of books, often from their youth. Gervais Phinn is adamant that teachers must know books: *There is no short cut, no easy answer, no definitive book list. Teachers need to have read the books they present to children, they need to select them with care and knowledge* (Harrison and Coles, 1995, p55).

Jacqui's decision to use her class texts while having a more informal approach to sharing and recommending books seems to be a sensible balance between books chosen for analysis and those to be enjoyed in a more relaxed way. Her children were very much focused on 'popular' reads but had little variety in their reading 'diet'. It is the teacher's job to ensure there is enough variety on the reading menu to enable children to make an informed choice and not be afraid of the unknown (Waugh and Jolliffe, 2008).

Renowned authors, including David Almond, have expressed that children are often directed to celebrity authors and ghostwriters, which he feels leaves children 'short-changed' when it comes to studying literature (Rudgard, 2017). Joanna Harris echoes Almond by saying *celebrity authors are the equivalent of the McDonald's Happy Meal. OK once in a while, perhaps, but not the everyday, varied diet a healthy child needs to flourish and grow* (Rudgard, 2017). There have been many trends for books which have shown authors or genres to be fashionable, or unfashionable, for a time. As an NQT, I distinctly remember an Ofsted inspector telling me there were too many Enid Blyton books in our library. Children's author Neil Gaiman remonstrates that there are no bad books and that all reading is a step towards literacy; if they enjoy reading a book, no adult should tell them that their particular book is 'wrong' (Gaiman, 2013). So, does it matter *what* children are reading?

CASE STUDY

Nicky felt that Charlie, a pupil in her Year 5 class who loved all sports, *needed to read more*, which she was sure would help him to improve his writing. She felt that he did not make the most of the quiet reading time in school and should 'focus' more. Charlie, however, insisted that he did read every day. His parents read aloud to him and his sister every evening from a children's novel and then he would independently read his football magazine (which was delivered every week). He also enjoyed reading blogs and reviews on the internet of various footballers and sporting achievements. He did not enjoy reading at school, however, as he found the books *boring*.

Case study reflections

- Would you describe Charlie as an engaged reader?
- What could Nicky do to support Charlie to 'read more'?

Choice: The impact of a variety of texts on the reader

RESEARCH FOCUS: MOTIVATING CHILDREN TO READ

Edmunds and Bauserman (2006) undertook a study to investigate what motivated a group of primary age children to read, believing that motivation and attainment in reading are linked. They focused on six areas of questions for children, including:

1. Which factors excite you to read narrative?
2. Which factors excite you to read non-fiction books?
3. Which factors get you excited about reading in general?
4. Who/what are the sources of any reading referrals?
5. Who/what are the sources of reading motivation?
6. What are the actions of those who motivate you?

(Edmunds and Bauserman, 2006)

The key findings are shown in Figure 3.1.

Why readers selected expository text:	**Why readers selected narrative text:**	**Sources of book referrals:**
1. Knowledge gained 2. Choice 3. Personal interests	1. Personal interest 2. Characteristic of books 3. Choice	1. School library 2. Teachers 3. Family members 4. Peers
Why readers selected reading in general:	**Actions of others:**	**Sources of motivation:**
1. Characteristic of books 2. Knowledge gained	1. Buying or giving books 2. Reading to children 3. Sharing books	1. Family members 2. Teachers 3. Themselves

Figure 3.1   Reading motivation: the six categories that motivate children to read

Adapted from Kathryn M. Edmunds and Kathryn L. Bauserman (2006) *What Teachers Can Learn About Reading Motivation through Conversations with Children.*

This study reflects the importance that both book choice and the availability of a variety of texts has on the motivation of the reader. When responding to questions about book choice, personal interest and being able to choose their own book were the most frequent responses: 84 per cent of the children in the study had chosen the book themselves while 14 per cent had chosen it based on a recommendation. In terms of recommendation, teachers and mothers were the persons most likely to introduce a book to them. Thinking back to Charlie in Year 5, with a wide variety of texts and good subject knowledge around them, it should not be too difficult for Nicky to introduce Charlie to a wider range of books he might like, based around his interest. Engaging parents in reading in school via parent reading workshops, reading coffee mornings and weekly book recommendations would also support the reading relationship between school and home.

List of possible challenging texts for Key Stage 2

Modern fiction

- *El Deafo*, Cece Bell. A graphic novel from the viewpoint of a deaf girl. Perfect for unpicking empathy around the attitudes towards the protagonist.

- *Letters from the Lighthouse*, Emma Carroll.

- *Love that Dog*, Sharon Creech. An intriguing structure, as it is all in first-person narrative. Is it poetry or prose? Links to a variety of poetry too.

- *The Terrible Thing That Happened to Barnaby Brocket*, John Boyne.

- *Wonder*, RJ Palacio.

- *The Boy Who Swam with Piranhas*, Oliver Jeffers. A moving story about an orphan boy who runs away with the fair. Themes are family/friendship/society's view of the travelling community.

- *The Rest of Us Just Live Here*, Patrick Ness. A very complex story with two narratives alongside each other.

- *Tin*, Padraig Kenny. A modern fairy tale which is set in a mechanical world. Consider friendship, courage and human identity in a world where machines have taken over.

- *Rooftoppers*, Katherine Rundell.

Picture books

- *The Viewer*, Gary Crew and Shaun Tan. A fascinating book with the most amazing illustrations, comparing how the world is viewed through history. There are so many interpretations on each page. The vocabulary is sophisticated, with a variety of grammar and punctuation to meet Y6 standards. Themes include the impact of man, progress and existence.

- *Footpath Flowers*, Jon Arno Lawson. This book has no words, so the focus is on the poignant illustrations and use of colour. Themes include parent–child relationships/death.

- *The Island*, Armin Greder. A powerful picture book addressing the themes of xenophobia and human rights.

- *The Sleeper and the Spindle*, Neil Gaiman and Chris Riddell.

Poetry

- *Moon Juice: Poems for Children*, Kate Wakeling. An absorbing collection of poetry addressing themes around childhood pressures.

- *Where My Wellies Take Me*, Michael Morpurgo. A journey through poetry and sketches.

- *The Noisy Classroom*. Ieva Flamingo.

- *Give the Ball to the Poet: A New Anthology of Caribbean Poetry*, edited by Georgie Horrell, Aisha Spencer and Morag Styles, illustrated by Jane Ray.

- *Falling Out of the Sky: Poems about Myths and Monsters*, edited by Rachel Piercey and Emma Wright.

- *Overheard in a Tower Block*, Joseph Coelho.

Classic fiction

- *Alice's Adventures in Wonderland*, Lewis Carroll.

- *The Secret Garden*, Frances Hodgson Burnett.

Myths and legends

- *The Legend of Podkin One-Ear*, Kieran Larwood. A beautifully written modern legend with all the ingredients of a traditional one. Strong female characters and terrifying villains. The narrative includes flashbacks.

- *The Polar-Bear Explorers' Club*, Alex Bell.

- *The 1,000-Year-Old Boy*, Ross Welford.

Other cultures

- *Welcome to Nowhere*, Elizabeth Laird. Syria's unfolding story through the eyes of 12-year-old Omar. Themes are war/refugees/home.

- *The Journey*, Francesca Sanna. The illustrations here echo the feelings as these refugees flee their country.

- *Unarranged Marriage*, Bali Rai. Themes around traditional values and family expectations.

- *Refugee Boy*, Benjamin Zephaniah.

Non-fiction

This should depend on what the children's interests are, but a few recommendations can be found below:

- *Young, Gifted and Black: Meet 52 Black Heroes from Past and Present*, Jamia Wilson and Andrew Pippins. Promote discussion with this collection of diverse and inspirational figures from past and present, including Serena Williams and Stevie Wonder.

- *The Street Beneath My Feet*, Charlotte Gullian. A fold-out book which takes you on a journey underground. Lots of layers to be explored.

Assessment

Jacqui's case study presented one teacher's journey of assessing her own subject knowledge in terms of meeting the needs of her children. The following questions are a good place to start for teachers wishing to assess their own knowledge around teachers' texts.

On a personal level:

- Do you know what your children are reading?

- Are the books able to challenge the readers?

- Do you have opportunities to talk to your children about their book choices or preferences?

- Are you able to make recommendations to your children based on their interests?

- Do you know where to access ideas for book lists/what's new etc.?

- How do you select quality texts to use in the classroom?

At whole-school level:

- How is a positive ethos around reading at school created?

- Do pupils have access to a wide range of books in school or through external opportunities such as the library/library service?

- Are there opportunities through school for children to discuss their reading?

- Are parents involved in reading in any way?

At book level:

- Can the reader apply their own interpretations to the text?

- Are the themes or author's voice challenging the reader to consider areas they may be unfamiliar with?

- Is the vocabulary accessible yet challenging for the reader, offering imagery they can explore?

- Is the sentence structure complex enough to challenge the reader at times?

- Is the narrative structure or cohesion between paragraphs particularly thought-provoking?

CHAPTER SUMMARY

Throughout this chapter we have looked at why a variety of challenging texts is important not only for children's interest and engagement, but to support progress and develop vital comprehension skills where children can unpick layers of meaning. Key consideration has been given to the teacher knowing the children as individuals, and to ensure they are offered books that they can relate to. This will eventually lead to trust and a willingness to step out of their reading comfort zone. Teachers are fundamental in supporting children with their book choices and should make every effort to stay abreast of a wide choice of texts.

Further reading

Books for keeps

A fabulous website which reviews children's books and has author and illustrator interviews. It also indicates suitable age ranges for books and offers the latest headlines from all the reputable children's book awards.

BookTrust

This website also reviews books, but it has a great collection of books based around themes.

Waugh, D, Neaum, S and Waugh, R (2013) *Children's literature in primary schools*, Transforming Primary QTS Series. London: Sage.

Join (or start!) a teachers' reading group such as Reading Teachers = Reading Children, Cheltenham Literature Festival.

References

Almond, D (2009) *Skellig*. London: Hodder.

Chambers, A (2011) *Tell Me: Children reading and talk*. Stroud: Thimble Press.

Clark, C and Rumbold, K (2006). *Reading for Pleasure: A research overview*. London: National Literacy Trust.

Cremin, T, Mottram, M, Collins, F, Powell, S and Safford, K (2009) Teachers as readers: Building communities of readers, *Literacy*, *43* (1): 11–19.

Cremin, T, Mottram, M, Powell, S, Collins, R and Safford, K (2014). *Building Communities of Engaged Readers: Reading for pleasure*. London: Routledge.

Department for Education (DfE) (2013) *The national curriculum in England: Framework for Key Stages 1 to 4*. London: DfE.

Dombey, H (2010) *Teaching Reading: What the evidence says*. Leicester: UKLA.

Edmunds, K and Bauserman, K (2006) What teachers can learn about reading motivation through conversations with children: The reading teacher, *International Reading Association*, *59* (5): 414–24.

Gaiman, N (2013) *Reading and obligation*, The Reading Agency lecture. Available: **https://readin gagency.org.uk/news/blog/neil-gaiman-lecture-in-full.html**

Gallagher, K (2004) *Deeper Reading: Comprehending challenging texts*. Portland, ME: Stenhouse Publishers.

Harrison, C and Coles, M (eds) (1992) *The Reading for Real Handbook*. London: Routledge.

Hoffman, J, Teale, WH and Yokota, J (2015) The book matters! Choosing narrative children's literature to support read aloud discussion of complex texts in the early grades, *Young Children*, *70*: 48–15.

Horowitz, A (2015) *Stormbreaker*. London: Walker Books.

Horton, S, Beattie, L and **Bingle, B** (2015) *Lessons in Teaching Reading Comprehension in Primary School*. London: Learning Matters.

Lawson, JA (2015) *Footpath Flowers*. London: Walker.

Morpurgo, M (2004) *Private Peaceful*. London: HarperCollins.

O'Neill, K (2011) Reading pictures: developing visual literacy for greater comprehension, *Reading Teacher*, *65* (3): 214–23.

Rudgard, O (2017) Authors turn on World Book Day for choosing too many works by celebrities: Angry writers complain that stars' stories are giving a 'false impression' of children's literature today, *Daily Telegraph*, 3 October.

Shanahan, T, Fisher, D and Frey, N (2012) The challenge of challenging text, *Educational Leadership*, *69* (6): 58–62.

Waugh, D and Jolliffe, W (2008) *English 3–11: A guide for teachers*. Oxon.: Routledge.

Waugh, D, Neaum, S and Waugh, R (2013) *Children's Literature in Primary Schools*, Transforming Primary QTS Series. London: Sage.

Welford, R (2018) *The 1,000-year-old Boy*. London: HarperCollins.

Williams, R (1986) Top ten principles for teaching reading, *ELT Journal*, *40* (1): 42–5.

4
ACCESSING TEXTS

(Continued)

- maintain positive attitudes to reading and an understanding of what they read by:
    o continuing to read and discuss an increasingly wide range of fiction, poetry, plays, non-fiction and reference books or textbooks
    o identifying and discussing themes and conventions in and across a wide range of writing
    o making comparisons within and across books
- understand what they read by:
    o checking that the book makes sense to them, discussing their understanding and exploring the meaning of words in context
    o asking questions to improve their understanding
    o drawing inferences such as inferring characters' feelings, thoughts and motives from their actions, and justifying inferences with evidence
    o predicting what might happen from details stated and implied
    o summarising the main ideas drawn from more than one paragraph, identifying key details that support the main ideas
    o identifying how language, structure and presentation contribute to meaning
- discuss and evaluate how authors use language, including figurative language, considering the impact on the reader
- participate in discussions about books that are read to them and those they can read for themselves, building on their own and others' ideas and challenging views courteously
- explain and discuss their understanding of what they have read, including through formal presentations and debates, maintaining a focus on the topic and using notes where necessary
- provide reasoned justifications for their views

Spoken Language

Pupils should be taught to:

- ask relevant questions to extend their understanding and knowledge
- use relevant strategies to build their vocabulary

(DfE, 2013)

What do we mean by accessing texts?

At Key Stage 2, the National Curriculum states that an emphasis should be on teaching reading to those pupils who are still unable to read to ensure they are 'secondary ready' (DfE, 2013). This, of course, generally means in terms of decoding. *"By the beginning of year 5, pupils should be able to read aloud a wider range of poetry and books written at an age-appropriate interest level with accuracy and at a reasonable speaking pace. They should be able to read most words effortlessly and to work out how to pronounce unfamiliar written words with increasing automaticity. If the pronunciation sounds unfamiliar, they should ask for help in determining both the meaning of the word and how to pronounce it correctly"* (DfE, 2013. P31).

For most pupils, however, reading at this stage will be focusing less on the decoding of words and more on the further development of comprehension skills. Although of course both skills are needed to read successfully, make sense of a text and understand it, these two areas can develop at different rates. Decoding is more of a focus at the beginning stages of reading, whilst comprehension development is life-long; children move from learning to read to reading to learn (Rose, 2006). This is reflected in the National Curriculum; it is divided into two areas: word reading and comprehension. As the curriculum moves chronologically from Year one to Year six, gradually, the number of comprehension objectives increase as the number of word objectives decrease. There may be an assumption that once children have reached a certain 'level' of reading, especially when they are able to decode independently and read aloud fluently, that they may not need support. However, children at all levels need support to deepen their understanding of a text - to access the layers of meaning, especially as the texts they read should have an appropriate level of challenge (see Chapter 3 for further reading around challenging texts). To continue to develop their reading skills, essentially their comprehension skills, children must have the ability to make connections between new vocabulary in the text, the context of that vocabulary and their own previous experience (Clarke *et al.* 2013). As this book is aimed at developing readers at Key Stage 2, this chapter will look at the skills and strategies needed by children to access challenging texts and how this will enhance the likelihood of children choosing challenging texts to independently read themselves, both for interest and pleasure and for information.

RESEARCH FOCUS: MODELS OF READING COMPREHENSION

There are several models that demonstrate the skills needed for readers to develop comprehension. The Simple View of Reading (Gough and Tunmer, 1986) (Figure 4.1) as advocated by The Rose Review (Rose, 2006), is perhaps the most well known in schools and focuses on the view that both decoding skills and language skills are needed to successfully comprehend texts. This model suggests that both elements are the foundation for reading but can be taught separately; a child may have strengths in only one of the two areas and teaching and intervention should be targeted to develop the area as needed. Support may focus on the language comprehension through vocabulary work or on the process of decoding (through phonics, for example). Only then can the child fully access (or comprehend) a text (Catts and Adlof, 2006). The diagram (Figure 4.1) enables teachers to 'plot' where the children in their class might be placed in terms of good language comprehension skills and word recognition, allowing for focused teaching in that area.

The Construction-integration model (Kintsch and Rawson, 2005 in Clarke, Truelove et al. 2013)

Updated in 2005, Kintsch and Rawson's Construction-integration model takes a slightly different view that suggests reading comprehension is a combination of the information given in the text and the readers' own general knowledge and personal experiences that they bring to the text (Clarke, Truelove *et al*, 2013). This model (Fig 4.2) proposes that the reader uses their own

(Continued)

(Continued)

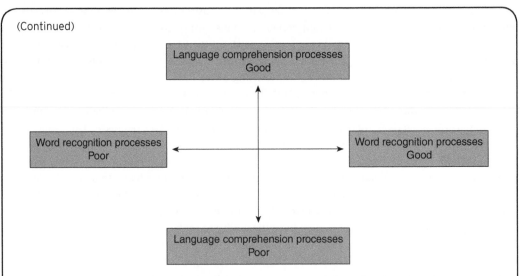

Figure 4.1   The Simple View of Reading (Gough and Tunmer, 1986)

experiences to build up a mental image, or even a personal relationship with the text as they read, continually adding to or refining meaning as the text develops. Alongside this personal experience is the information provided by the text which they call a 'text base'. This text base is formed from three levels: linguistic (recognising word meaning); microstructure (understanding words within a larger context) and macrostructure (looking at a deeper level. For example, themes). The reader combines this text base with their own knowledge and experience; this then forms an individual response (Clarke, Truelove *et al*, 2013). It is this 'macrostructure' which leads to the depth of understanding - the area of teaching critical to develop higher levels of reading.

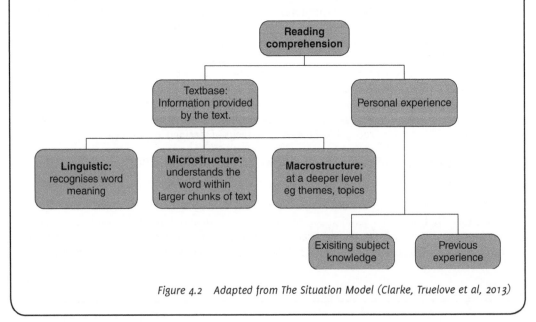

Figure 4.2   Adapted from The Situation Model (Clarke, Truelove et al, 2013)

Whichever model you look at, each one has vocabulary at the heart of accessing a text. The National Curriculum endorses this idea with an emphasis on vocabulary: *"teachers should continue to emphasise pupils' enjoyment and understanding of language, especially vocabulary, to support their reading and writing"* (DfE, 2013, p32). It goes on to state that by the end of year 6, children should *"be able to reflect their understanding of the audience for and purpose of their writing by selecting appropriate vocabulary and grammar"* and *"understand nuances in vocabulary choice and age-appropriate, academic vocabulary. This involves consolidation, practice and discussion of language"* (DfE, 2013, p32).

Content domain at KS2

This link to language and vocabulary and its position in supporting the development of comprehension has impacted upon primary schools. A useful document is the English reading test framework (STA, 2016) which supports assessment in primary schools. Developed as a guide for test developers to inform them of the content at the end of both primary key stages, rather than a guide for teachers, the content domains nevertheless give an insight into the key areas expected for children to meet the expected standards. (See Figure 4.3)

2a	give / explain the meaning of words in context
2b	retrieve and record information / identify key details from fiction and non-fiction
2c	summarise main ideas from more than one paragraph
2d	make inferences from the text / explain and justify inferences with evidence from the text
2e	predict what might happen from details stated and implied
2f	identify / explain how information / narrative content is related and contributes to meaning as a whole
2g	identify / explain how meaning is enhanced through choice of words and phrases
2h	make comparisons within the text

Figure 4.3   The KS2 Content Domain (STA, 2016)

The increase in the expectation in vocabulary is clear; 2a and 2g focus explicitly on vocabulary knowledge. In fact, in the 2017 SATs paper, 22% of the questions focused on areas of vocabulary knowledge (content domain 2a and 2g). (https://www.gov.uk/government/publications/key-stage-2-tests-2017-english-reading-test-materials contains the mark scheme with reference to the content domain). 44% of the 2017 paper was based around questions that required inference (2d); again, this links closely to comprehension and accessing the text.

The 2017 test saw vocabulary questions such as:

A Siamese cat crouched on a tree branch, peering down at Gaby with brilliant blue eyes.

Which word is closest in meaning to crouched?

- *balanced*

- *squatted*

- *trembled*

- *pounced*

Not only did this directly test the pupils' knowledge of vocabulary, but to access the test itself, children needed to be able to independently read and understand a range of words which were more highly demanding than in previous years. This included words or phrases such as: 'universal rule', 'rhinestone', 'manoeuvre', 'outlawed', 'comparatively', 'arcs of radiating lines', 'savouring', 'sluicing' and 'supernovae'. The increased difficulty of these tests reflected the increased rigour demanded by the National Curriculum 2014, and many schools took this as an opportunity to re-examine the strategies and pedagogies used to develop comprehension.

Why is vocabulary so important?

At its most simple, defining 'vocabulary' is the understanding of a word, but poor vocabulary has far reaching implications. Snowling (Oxford University Press, 2018, p6) explains, *Language is the foundation of education and is vital for social and emotional development. Children with poor oral language are at high risk of poor literacy and hence, educational failure. They can also experience difficulty in communicating to make friends, to engage in activities and to express their feelings,* Nation (Oxford University Press, 2018, p5), concurs *Regardless of the causes, low levels of vocabulary set limits on literacy, understanding, learning the curriculum and can create a downward spiral of poor language which begins to affect all aspects of life.* Individuals never stop developing vocabulary (Cain and Oakhill, in Oxford University Press, 2018) and it is a huge predictor of how far children will succeed in school and beyond (Block and Mangieri, 2006; Hohm *et al*, 2007). There is a great deal of research into vocabulary and its importance in developing comprehension, which impacts on being able to access a text. According to Byrnes and Wasik (cited in Jalango, 2011), children need to learn at least 5 to 6 new words a day, 38 a week, 2000 a year and 10000 by the age of 6 in to become proficient readers. From birth onwards, more vocabulary is 'collected' (Carter, 2014) as a child begins to understand the sounds which become words and the meanings associated with them, until eventually the word can be recognised in print. This emphasises the importance of developing language from a child's early years, but of course the same applies to our able readers; opportunities to experience and develop a higher level of vocabulary must be provided.

RESEARCH FOCUS: HOW IS VOCABULARY DEVELOPED?

Armbruster et al (2001) suggest that vocabulary can be learned both indirectly and directly:

1. Indirectly in three ways: daily language use; adults reading to children and children reading independently. This is where opportunities to talk and a wide range of reading material is beneficial.

2.   Directly: specific vocabulary teaching is needed alongside this indirect learning. They suggest that through specific word instruction and teaching word-learning strategies, children's vocabulary will continue to develop.

Hiebert and Kamil (2005, p2) describe two forms of vocabulary learning: in print, where the reader reads and writes silently, and oral, where the reader reads aloud or hear words spoken. Echoing the reading models above, they go on to report that a child's oral vocabulary should be greater than its reading vocabulary, otherwise the reader will be unable to recognise the meaning of the word he has decoded, and good reading comprehension will not occur. As a reader becomes more skilled, the print then becomes the main vehicle (the context) for learning new vocabulary (Hiebert and Kamil, 2005, p2).

Other research suggests that there is a need for teaching vocabulary explicitly. This will enhance vocabulary needed for key topics, understanding narratives or to bridge the gap for any children not exposed to a language-rich environment (William Nagy in Hiebert and Kamil, p29). Although this of course takes time and cannot be done with every word. Ford-Connors and Paratore (2015) agree that explicit vocabulary instruction in schools does have a significant impact on developing children's vocabulary, although this should not be solely using definition or dictionary methods but must be through an active process (Wright and Cervetti, 2016, p206). How this then impacts on comprehension is not so clear, although Nagy (2005) posits that they are both reciprocal; a child with a wide vocabulary will have access to more texts which he can comprehend. This access to wider texts will then introduce the same child to a wider vocabulary; therefore, vocabulary and comprehension work reciprocally (Nagy, 2005, p 34). See Figure 4.4.

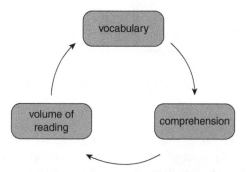

Fig 4.4   A reciprocal model of vocabulary and reading comprehension (Nagy, 2005)

Beck and McKeown (in Hiebert and Kamil, 2005) developed '3 tier words.' They suggested that there are three key areas of vocabulary (see Figure 4.5) and that by focusing vocabulary teaching on the tier 2 words, those words that are complex but useful and may just be out of their grasp, children will build a vocabulary that will be wider, challenging and more specific. In contrast, tier 1 words are rather simple, everyday words and tier 3 would be very subject specific. To increase access for your more experienced reader to an even wider range of texts, perhaps learning new vocabulary to represent a new or unknown concept or theme is the key. For example, introducing children to the idea of refugees will open up a host of themes and concepts (and therefore vocabulary) that are both

(Continued)

(Continued)

political and social (Armbruster *et al*, 2001). This is imperative for the critical literacy skills needed for readers to access texts at a deeper level. Critical Literacy *'encourages readers to be active participants in the reading process: to question, to dispute, and to examine power relations. It also asks us to second guess what we believe is true, ask harder and harder questions, see underneath, behind, and beyond the texts, see how these texts establish and use power over us, over others, on whose behalf, and in whose interest'.* (Molden, 2007, p50). Using a teacher focus on tier 2 words to explore the text and careful questioning, readers can really begin to explore the layers in a text.

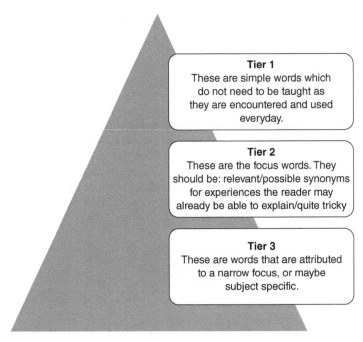

Tier 1
These are simple words which do not need to be taught as they are encountered and used everyday.

Tier 2
These are the focus words. They should be: relevant/possible synonyms for experiences the reader may already be able to explain/quite tricky

Tier 3
These are words that are attributed to a narrow focus, or maybe subject specific.

Figure 4.5   Demonstrating Beck's 3 Tier Model

Building on this research, Graves, Baumann *et al* (2014) suggested that a teacher should focus on a text and identify words that children may not know. The teacher should then decide which of those words should be taught by considering whether they are deemed:

1. Essential (imperative to understanding the text); Valuable (words that aren't essential to understand the text, but are useful);

2. Accessible (perhaps high-frequency words, or words that will support those with a limited vocabulary); or

3. Imported (these words enhance a reader's understanding but may not actually be in the text. For example, it might address themes or character traits).

(Graves, Baumann *et al*, 2014).

Again, the emphasis of this theory is that a wider vocabulary knowledge leads to easier access to, and comprehension of, the text.

CASE STUDY: SETTING THE SCENE FOR A WIDER VOCABULARY

Ethan was keen to make vocabulary more high profile in his teaching. He started every Monday by sharing a 'word of the week' which he either took from a relevant text, or from a word generator (try. https://en.oxforddictionaries.com/ or https://vocabularyninja.wordpress.com/). He would share the definition, put it into context and model orally with the children how it could be used. For example, 'bombastic', or 'side-kick'. Children were then challenged to orally use the word during the week and were rewarded with a house-point when they did. This really engaged the children and soon became very popular, resulting in children suggesting their own words, so he displayed them within a sentence on his wall. Ethan noticed that some children were also using the words in their writing, even after the week had moved on, so he would reward that too. Ethan also considered his own use of language and realised there were many opportunities to model a wider range of vocabulary (see David Reedy's chapter in Oxford University Press (2018)). As a result, he began to use language more precisely. For example, 'Look at the extract' became 'Consider the extract'; 'Has anyone got the answer?' became 'Have you reached a conclusion?' and 'explain' became 'justify' or 'clarify'; these subtle shifts caused Ethan to question his own use of vocabulary and raise his expectations of the pupils' word choices. He demonstrated the language that he was expecting from the children.

Ethan also concentrated on explicit modelling of synonyms and how words can be more carefully chosen to enhance meaning. As well as using thesauruses, Ethan focused more on the online tools that children were familiar with, such as using the synonym tool on 'Word'. He also had iPads out for the children to use during writing sessions, so they could access websites to explore synonyms (try www.thesaurus.com). As extension activities, children were encouraged to play vocabulary games on the iPads and with each other (for example, https://www.spellingcity.com/ or http://www.gamequarium.org/dir/Readquarium/Vocabulary/Synonyms/). Some of the children then reported that they had been playing these games at home too.

Gradually, children began to try out new words in different contexts and began to question words and share 'word stories' with Ethan and the class, setting each other word challenges such as:

* What is the longest word in the English language?
* What is the most recognised word across the world?
* Can you find a word with 3 vowels in a row?
* How are words 'invented'?
* How many words contain an 'x'?

The result was a genuine enthusiasm for exploring language which provided a foundation for more focused word work.

Case study reflections

* Is there a high standard of vocabulary expected by the class teacher and throughout the school? How are these standards demonstrated?
* Are quality examples of language modelled by the teacher and in the texts shared by the children?
* Are the children given opportunities to meet new words, discuss them and have fun with them?

RESEARCH FOCUS: THE WORD-GAP

In Ethan's case study, it is important to see that through a focus on language and some subtle changes of his own use of vocabulary, the vocabulary profile had been raised. Unfortunately, more and more research has commented on 'the word gap' – simply, children not knowing enough vocabulary. In its report, the Oxford University Press (2018) found that the number of children with a limited vocabulary is increasing. Half of the 473 primary teachers who took part in the survey stated that 49% of year 1 children had a limited vocabulary to such an extent that it affected their learning. 86% of the teachers also agreed that the children's limited vocabulary had an impact on children being able to access end of key stage tests, such as SATs.

CASE STUDY: FOCUSING ON VOCABULARY TO ACCESS A TEXT

Indira's school knew they had to refocus the teaching of developing vocabulary and comprehension across the school. She had a very mixed class of year 5 pupils, but she wanted them all to be able to access and enjoy the class reader - *Podkin One-ear* (Larwood, 2017) - a beautiful legend with many modern-day themes. Indira's priority was to try to develop the class's interest in words; how could she build on their current knowledge; excite them to want to gather a wider range of words; support them to find and use new words independently?

Prior to starting the novel, the class had talked around some of the ideas in the text, prompted by the blurb. They had started to collect key 'rabbit-themed' vocabulary. For example, warren, doe, flank, dewlap - all prompted by the children's current knowledge of rabbits and added to the word-wall. They had also discussed legends that they were aware of and key events or themes in a legend. For example, magic, bravery, honour. Previous to sharing the extract, (Figure 4.6) Indira had identified the words in italics as being the words the pupils may not know: *justice*, *mottled*, and *shard*. She displayed the words as the children came in in the morning and asked her pupils to discuss with their partners any prior knowledge of the words. Did they recognise the words? Did they sound like any words they had heard before?

With a final grinding squeal, the figure emerged and leapt from the tunnel to land in the warrior's circle.

The rabbits had all heard terrifying tales of the Gorm, but none had done the real thing *justice*.

This wasn't a rabbit anymore. If it ever had been, it was now something else entirely. A walking slab of metal and meat, pierced through with rusty thorns and nails. Its armour overlapped in sheets of jagged, dented iron; *mottled* with rust and splashes of dried crimson that looked very much like old blood.

Its head was completely covered by a helm, dotted all over with cruel, *shard*-like spikes and curved metal horns that almost scraped the ceiling. From the shadowy eye-slits, two dim scarlet pupils glowed; blank and mottled with rusty red veins.

Podkin was so scared, he wanted to cry. P18–19

Figure 4.6   Extract from The Legend of Podkin One-ear (Harwood, 2017)

She then gave them some phrases with the key word in:

- Malala believed there was no *justice* as to why she could not attend school in Pakistan, just because she was a girl.

- The over-ripe banana was *mottled* with yellow and brown stains.

- *Shards* of glass scattered from the broken mirror.

With a final grinding squeal, **What a horrible noise**.

the figure emerged and leapt from the tunnel **Figure? Is it human? It sounds like it's about to pounce. Why was it in a tunnel?**

to land in the warrior's circle. **'Warrior' sounds like its ready for a fight**.

The rabbits had all heard terrifying tales of the Gorm, **Is Gorm the species or name? It has a capital letter, so it sounds like a name. Terrifying? I knew it didn't sound good**.

but none had done the real thing justice. **Ah, justice. I know that means fair. So, the tales weren't fair - the Gorm is worse than terrifying! What is he going to do to the rabbits?**

Figure 4.7   Think aloud' demonstration of understanding the text.

Again, in pairs, the children discussed the meaning - did the context help? Why?

During the literacy lesson, Indira then used a 'Think aloud' strategy (Israel and Massey, 2005) for the first few sentences of the text, modelling how she used her knowledge to unpick the text, asking questions of the text to begin to make sense of it. She verbalised her own thinking and how she might work things out. (See Figure 4.7: italics are Indira's thoughts spoken aloud.) Indira then re-read the passage aloud, modelling how she could re-read parts for clarity.

Working in pairs, the children were then given a line from the remainder of the passage (Fig 4.6) which they could then 'investigate'. Their challenge was to either draw or translate (or both) what came to mind from their phrase. For example...

- a walking slab of metal and meat
- pierced through with rusty thorns and nails
- its armour overlapped in sheets of jagged, dented iron
- its head was completely covered with a helm

Each pair then had to feedback their interpretations, displaying them on the working wall. This gave the children support to completely analyse a short section before reading the whole passage.

Case study reflections

- Do you choose words to pre-teach before reading?
- How do you select these words?
- How do you provide opportunities for children to explore vocabulary?

Assessment

Indira's case study reflected how she had responded after considering her own teaching of comprehension and vocabulary. Probably prompted by the changes in the curriculum and the new tests, she realised that she needed to focus more widely on explicit modelling of strategies and finding new opportunities to meet and discuss new vocabulary. The following questions might help you reflect on your own practice.

- Are there opportunities for story-telling, where children can use props and puppets to make their own oral stories?

- Is morphology modelled as a strategy to work out the meaning of words? Is it built into any spelling work that might take place?

- Are children exposed to a wide range of vocabulary through the carefully chosen texts that you share with them (see chapter 3 for a wide choice of challenging texts)?

- Are there opportunities for pupils to talk? Are there prompts for discussion and hypothetical scenarios that invite talk?

- Do you play word games around homonyms/homophones/idioms/puns to excite and encourage exploration?

- Are there opportunities to use film or images in your teaching to introduce new vocabulary? This will support those pupils who may not be able to decode. It will also support able readers with new concepts.

- Does the whole school have high expectations of vocabulary? This could be modelled in discussion and day-to-day activities, with the focus on praising children for the rich use of spoken vocabulary.

CHAPTER SUMMARY

This chapter has considered the skills and strategies that children need to use, and teachers need to teach and model, for children to be able to access texts. With research underpinning this, the focus on developing vocabulary as an important tool in developing comprehension is apparent. This is crucial not just for emerging readers, but also for competent, able readers to continue to access the layers of the text.

Further reading

Oxford University Press (2018) *Why Closing the Word Gap Matters*. Oxford Language Report. Oxford: Oxford University Press.

For further case studies on developing vocabulary in the classroom, read: **Lane, Holly B; Allen, Stephanie Arriaza** (2010). The vocabulary-rich classroom: Modeling sophisticated word-use to promote word consciousness and vocabulary growth. *The Reading Teacher*, Vol 63(5): 362–370.

Reference

Armbruster, B. B. Lehr, F. Osborn, J. Adler, R. (2001). *Put reading first: the research building blocks for teaching children to read: kindergarten through grade 3*.[Washington, D.C.?]: National Institute for Literacy, National Institute of Child Health and Human Development, U.S. Dept. of Education.

Beck, I. L., McKeown, M. G., and Kucan, L. (2005). Choosing words to teach. In E. Hiebert & M. Kamil (Eds.) *Teaching and Learning Vocabulary: Bringing research to practice* (pp. 207–222). Mahwah, NJ: Erlbaum.

Block, C.C. and Mangieri, J.N. (2006) *The Vocabulary Enriched Classroom*. New York: Scholastic.

Carter, J. (2014) cited in Ethanliffe, W., Waugh, D., Allott, K. *Primary English for Trainee Teachers*, London: Sage.

Catts, H. W. and Adlof, S. (2006) Language Deficits in Poor Comprehenders: A Case for The Simple View of Reading. *Journal of Speech and Language and Hearing Research. 49*: 278–293

Clarke, Paula J; Truelove, Emma, Hulme, Charles, Snowling, Margaret J. (2013). *Developing Reading Comprehension*. New York: Wiley & Sons, Incorporated.

Clarke, Paula J; Truelove, Emma, Hulme, Charles, Snowling, Margaret J (2010) Ameliorating Children's Reading-Comprehension Difficulties. A Randomized Controlled Trial. *Psychological Science* 8:1106–1116

Department for Education (DfE) (2013) *The National Curriculum in England: Framework document*. London: DfE.

Ford-Connors, E., and Paratore, J.R. (2015). Vocabulary instruction in fifth grade and beyond: Sources of word learning and productive contexts for development. *Review of Educational Research*, 85(1), 50–91.

Gough, P. B., and Tunmer, W. E. (1986). Decoding, reading, and reading disability. *Remedial and Special Education, 7*, 6–10.

Graves, M.F, Baumann, J.F., Blachowicz, C.L.Z., Manyak, P., Bates, A., Cieply, C., Davis, J.R. and Von Gunten, H. (2014) Words, words everywhere but which ones do we teach? *The Reading Teacher, 67*(5), 333–346.

Hiebert, Elfrieda H; Kamil, Michael L. (2005) *Teaching and Learning Vocabulary: Bringing research to practice*. Mahwah, New Jersey: Lawrence Erlbaum Associates.

Hohm, E., Jennen-Steinmetz, C., Schmidt, M.H. and **Hancht, M**. (2007) Language development at ten months. *European Child & Adolescent Psychiatry, 16*(3), 149–156.

Israel, S. E. and Massey, D. (2005) Metacognitive Think-alouds: using a gradual release model with middle school students, in S.E. Israel, C.C. Block, K. L. Bausermann and K. K. Kinnucan-Welsch (eds) **Metacognition in Literacy Learning: Theory, assessment instruction and professional development.** Mahwah, NJ: Lawrence Erlbaum.

Jalango, M. R., and Sobolak, M. J. (2011). Supporting young children's vocabulary growth: The challenges, the benefits, and evidence-based strategies. *Early Childhood Education Ethanurnal*, New York 38:6:421–429.

Larwood, K. (2017) *The Legend of Podkin One-ear*, London: Faber & Faber.

Molden, K. (2007) Critical literacy, the right answer for the reading classroom: strategies to move beyond comprehension for reading improvement. *Reading Improvement, 44*(1), 50.

Nagy, W (2005) *Why vocabulary instruction needs to be long term and comprehensive*, in Hiebert, Elfrieda H; Kamil, Michael L. (eds) *Teaching and Learning Vocabulary: Bringing Research to Practice*. Mahwah, New Jersey: Lawrence Erlbaum Associates.

Oxford University Press, (2018) *Why Closing the Word Gap Matters*. Oxford Language Report. Oxford: Oxford University Press.

Rose, J. (2006) *Independent Review of Early Reading: Final report*. London: DfE.

STA (2016) Key stage 2 English reading test framework: national curriculum tests from 2016. *This document is available for download on the GOV.UK* website at www.gov.uk/sta.

STA (2017) 2017 key stage 2 English reading test mark schemes. Available online at https://assets. publishing.service.gov.uk/government/uploads/system/uploads/attachment_data/file/614598/ STA177732e_2017_key_stage_2_English_reading_mark_schemes.pdf

Wright, Tanya S and Cervetti, Gina N. (2016) A systematic review of the research on vocabulary instruction that impacts text comprehension. *Reading Research Quarterly*, *52*(2) pp. 203–226

5

ANALYSING TEXTS

CHAPTER OBJECTIVES

This chapter will allow you to achieve the following outcomes:

- Have an awareness of the research associated with analysing texts;
- Understand some of the challenges associated with teaching how to analyse texts;
- Know how to plan for textual analysis;
- Know how to teach analysis through discussion work and questioning.

LINKS TO THE TEACHERS' STANDARDS

Working through this chapter will help you meet the following standards:

1. Set high expectations which inspire, motivate and challenge pupils
2. Promote good progress and outcomes by pupils
3. Demonstrate good subject and curriculum knowledge
4. Plan and teach well-structured lessons
5. Adapt teaching to respond to the strengths and needs of all pupils

LINKS TO THE NATIONAL CURRICULUM

Years 5 and 6 Programme of Study

Reading - comprehension

Pupils should be taught to:

(Continued)

(Continued)

- understand what they read by:

  o checking that the book makes sense to them, discussing their understanding and exploring the meaning of words in context

  o asking questions to improve their understanding

  o drawing inferences such as inferring characters' feelings, thoughts and motives from their actions, and justifying inferences with evidence

  o predicting what might happen from details stated and implied

  o summarising the main ideas drawn from more than one paragraph, and identifying key details that support the main ideas

  o identifying how language, structure and presentation contribute to meaning

- discuss and evaluate how authors use language, including figurative language, considering the impact on the reader

- participate in discussions about books that are read to them and those they can read for themselves, building on their own and others' ideas and challenging views courteously

- explain and discuss their understanding of what they have read, including through formal presentations and debates, maintaining a focus on the topic and using notes where necessary

- provide reasoned justifications for their views.

(DfE, 2013)

What do we mean by analysing texts?

In teachers' pursuit of developing more able and critical readers, they are inevitably drawn to the consideration of analysis of texts and what this looks like in the primary classroom. There is an implicit understanding that the ability to analyse texts is linked to 'being a good reader' and that this skill will be honed at secondary school in order to achieve at GCSE level – not just in English but in a range of text-based studies. So where do we start with planning to teach analysis? There are numerous sources of research which explore how children comprehend texts and to a certain degree this includes the skill of analysis. However, there is limited literature which focuses solely on *analysis* of texts.

If we take the meaning of analysis to indicate a detailed examination, this would necessarily include questioning 'how?' and 'why?' a text was written. This will move us towards a close reading of the text in order to explore these basic questions and to conclude with an assertion of an opinion on a text. In terms of our planning for teaching, this premise allows for a more structured approach which sits within our understanding of reading comprehension. It has been suggested (Brown, 2008) that a collaborative learning environment will enable children to build up their reading competencies over time moving them towards independence and being good readers (Horton *et al.*, 2015). At this point it is pertinent to remember the correlation between enjoyment of reading and attainment as explored in Chapter 2 (Clark and de Zoysa, 2011; Twist *et al.*, 2012). Thus considering how we initially choose a text and plan to engage the children is of the utmost importance.

CASE STUDY: PLANNING TO TEACH TEXTUAL ANALYSIS

This case study explores how a teacher's planning resulted in:

- an increase in pupil engagement in text;
- deeper analysis during close reading;
- a renewal of creativity around responses to text.

Hayley was keen to extend the analytical thinking of the pupils in her Year 5 class. They were responsive to new approaches and enjoyed literacy lessons. She had used guided reading during the autumn term to support lower ability readers and had found that the relationships with pupils had improved alongside their confidence when tackling new texts. She was confident in planning for a whole-class text but had reflected on how she might choose a more challenging text and bridge the gap between the pupils' current reading ability and a closer reading with an in-depth understanding of the craft behind the text. She recognised that the link between pupil engagement and their confidence in facing this new challenge was significant. Therefore she spent some time thinking about the interests and backgrounds of her children alongside the types of texts available to her which would allow her to extend their reading stamina and deepen their analytical skills.

Having decided upon *Holes* by Louis Sachar, Hayley now thought about the first encounter with the text. Which would be the best way to 'hook' her pupils and to gain their trust in the text? She thought carefully about the more active approaches to text which would enable her to explore small segments of a larger, more challenging text. She considered active approaches through drama to facilitate collaborative learning and improved comprehension (Horton *et al.*, 2015). This reduced the need for a 'correct' answer as the pupils had the freedom to consider their first response to the character of Stanley and to question each other about the reasons for their thoughts (Pressley, 2000).

Building children's interest and confidence allowed Hayley to increase the degree of close reading which followed. Her intricate questioning of characters' motivations and relationships was timely as the pupils had built a vested interest in and understanding of them. They felt empowered to experiment with new ways of thinking and responding within a safe learning environment. Hayley was surprised by the level of commitment that the pupils showed towards the text and was able to further build on this as the unit of work progressed. It changed the way she approached planning for reading in the subsequent year as she made more explicit links between active approaches to reading and the resultant progression in analytical skills.

Case study reflections

- How do you plan for active approaches to texts in order to preface close reading?
- In what ways does teacher questioning feature in this and enhance the learning experience?
- What might pupils say about the flexibility of this approach from their point of view?

The importance of analysing texts

As outlined above, the ability to delve into texts and critically examine them underpins what teachers are searching for when they plan for analysis of texts. It is the robust nature with which children feel confident enough to dive into such activities that contributes to this. With careful nurturing of comprehension and questioning skills, pupils will become adept at managing new and unfamiliar texts. They will be used to seeing a range of texts and being encouraged to discuss them and share ideas. The ethos for reading will have an impact on this confidence and children will approach new texts with less trepidation or anxiety about 'getting it right'. It is within this safe reading ethos that the notion of exploratory talk comes to the fore (Mercer and Dawes, 2008) as it allows pupils to explore texts collaboratively to find a shared meaning and understanding. Not only does this contribute to greater depth of understanding but it precipitates further questioning of texts moving children towards literary analysis – the 'why?' and 'how?' behind the text.

RESEARCH FOCUS: COLLABORATIVE LEARNING THROUGH EXPLORATORY TALK

The benefits of collaborative learning and exploratory talk are well documented (Alexander, 2004; Mercer and Dawes, 2008; Rojas-Drummond *et al.*, 2014) and pivotal in many teachers' experimental development of reading stamina in the primary classroom (Horton *et al.*, 2015). The premise has underpinned developmental work for some time and yet with the pressures of a new curriculum and formalised testing, the benefits have sometimes been overridden by time constraints. In these instances space and time have worked against such approaches (Coultas, 2016). Research by Coultas (2016) found that the pedagogical benefits of exploring and probing texts through talk for learning worked in direct opposition to the pressure of performativity and targets.

These tensions may sometimes result in teachers feeling that they do not have enough time to plan for talk about texts and yet the foundations for critical reading can be built through such activities. It is at this creative stage that pupils are more likely to open up to the text and consider their immediate reactions to a character, the setting or a dramatic moment. If this is well-structured at the planning stage and has a clear focus in the teacher's mind, then the children's engagement with one another will be both constructive and increasingly critical. Given the time to explore, share and collaborate encourages children to build upon talk (Brett, 2016). They will want to question and compare what they think (Pressley, 2000) and at this point the teacher can eavesdrop to assess progress or intervene to challenge or support.

The point at which the teacher moves into more in-depth questioning about the text has been successfully scaffolded and the pupils are well placed to cope with greater rigour (McGuinn, 2014).

CASE STUDY: USING EXPLORATORY TALK IN THE CLASSROOM

Jake's Year 6 class had engaged in exploratory talk around texts throughout KS2. Having read a modern text as a class reader, he was now keen to offer greater literary challenge through exploring a nineteenth-century text. After careful consideration of the interests of the class and how to engage some more reluctant male readers, he decided that a gothic themed approach would be appropriate. Taking into account the length of full texts and time constraints, he moved towards a segmented range of extracts which were linked, not only by the gothic theme, but also the literary focus of setting. In so doing, he was planning for and modelling how to structure analytical approaches to text. There was also the opportunity to build the foundation of comparison skills and intertextuality (see Chapter 7 for further guidance).

Jake decided on extracts from *Frankenstein* (Shelley), *Northanger Abbey* (Austen), *The Hound of the Baskervilles* (Conan Doyle) and *Wuthering Heights* (Brontë). He was focused at the planning stage to ensure that the chosen text extracts encouraged the children to explore the setting and connotations within the language so this gave him a clear scaffold for structured group work and questioning. This also facilitated the space in lesson time for pupils to explore their own responses to the literature and to form opinions about the writer's intentions. Through low-key, collaborative work, Jake would be ensuring that he was guiding them towards a closer reading as he questioned and challenged their responses.

Thinking about the benefits of collaborative learning (Alexander, 2004) assisted Jake in planning for group-based talk when first responding to the extracts. Any anxiety in dealing with more challenging text was alleviated through careful planning about how the text would be read. Jake opted for a teacher reading to begin with to ensure that this modelled the tone and also dealt with pronunciation of new or unfamiliar words. He then planned for groups to re-read the extracts with marks showing where they should stop and consider some key questions in the middle of the table. This broke up the heavy nature of the text and allowed some sequential processing of comprehension and predictions about the text. Key questions included:

- How does the time of day and weather make you feel as you read this extract?
- What words would your group use to describe the atmosphere? Prioritise the top three and be ready to explain your choices.
- By writing in first/third person narrative, what effect did this achieve?

Jake scaffolded this work by annotating some extracts for nominated groups. A lower-ability group had a shortened version of the extract and some sentences were already highlighted so that the children could go straight to the sentences which required closer reading. This ensured that the task was differentiated so that they accessed the exploratory and analytical skills required in the lesson rather than trying to find the sentence which was worthy of examination. Jake's long-term planning ensured that skim reading and retrieval of text was an ongoing skill for development with these pupils but did not want to deter them from higher-order thinking. In one group, he added a higher-ability pupil to direct the talk for the lower-ability pupils. This pupil had been briefed in advance and was aware that this was to develop her own speaking and listening skills, in particular taking a lead in group work.

Jake found that the children looked forward to the next piece of text and were responding well to the autonomy of exploring and proffering their interpretation of the atmosphere. The interest and excitement in the gothic nature of the texts led naturally to some contextual work around

(Continued)

(Continued)

the times the writers were living in and some of the common, cultural beliefs at the time. It was not long before the pupils were beginning to make their own links between texts and offer intuitive comparisons. Jake was then able to layer some further challenging questions into his planning to hone this interest into a more solid understanding of comparative skills. Some able pupils were asking for further reading recommendations while some pupils were making links to modern, gothic writing. The class as a whole was hooked into the theme and therefore felt safe as Jake increased the rigour and expectation of their close reading.

Case study reflections

- How do you plan for active approaches to new texts?
- How do you use collaborative approaches to develop exploratory talk and enhance reading stamina?
- What do you consider to be the benefits of collaborative approaches to the close reading of texts?

Close reading

Close reading is easily explained to children alongside skimming and scanning. Obviously, it involves getting closer to the text ... but how? What does this mean for the teacher? It requires time to plan for multiple readings of the text and focused questions which will unearth new meaning or insight for the children. It is this layering of investigation which will build a greater depth of understanding and therefore an ability to analyse the text (Brown and Kappes, 2012). The teaching of context and other scaffolds to support the overall comprehension of the text might be front loaded before the pupils begin the text. However, this limits the ability to explore and discuss which will facilitate close reading as outlined above. By thinking about how these scaffolds can be planned *during* the reading of the text, the teacher is supporting the pupils with a layered close reading. With each added layer comes new meaning and an ability to analyse.

One such scaffold will be questions. These should be planned in advance even if they are not all used. These are the structure behind the collaborative work, behind the paired or shared reading of the text rather than an independent comprehension exercise. Fisher and Frey (2014) found that some teachers tended to chunk their questions into three areas: *What does the text say? How does the text work? What does it mean?* (p279). Equally, the questions can follow Bloom's Taxonomy (1956) hierarchy of skills, beginning with literal understanding of the text and moving through increasingly more complex thinking skills which might require pupils to compare or justify alternative views. At this point, many teachers will introduce annotating the text to encourage pupils to think through their understanding thus far and to crystallise this in a word or two on a copy of the text (or electronically).

In addition to the scaffolding of close reading as described here, Fisher and Frey's research also showed that teachers tended to have contingency plans when teaching close reading. Following discussions

with teachers, they grouped these contingency plans into five areas: re-establishing the purpose, analysing questions to identify likely answer locations, prompting and cueing, modelling and analysing
annotations (p282). Many of these are regularly utilised teaching strategies, but it is interesting to see
them listed together as 'contingency methods' when teaching close reading. It is a reminder to teachers at the planning stage that there needs to be a degree of flexibility behind the plan and that pupils
will sometimes need to be redirected when undertaking this type of analytical work. It is helpful to
consider this explicitly as another set of sub-skills for teacher and pupil in tandem.

CASE STUDY

Referring back to Jake's planned unit of work on nineteenth-century gothic literature, we will now
focus on how he approached the close reading of the *Frankenstein* extract. He chose an extract
from the beginning of Chapter 5 when Frankenstein has just completed his monster and the
passage describes his reaction. It is ideal for considering the setting and the narrative voice of
Frankenstein as well as gaining an insight into his scientific motivations and moral and psychological reactions. Through careful planning of the reading and questioning, pupils can explore this passage and collaborate to make meaning together.

Jake chose a popular activity which required the children to draw (you could have a pre-drawn
outline of one) the monster and to ask the pupils to complete the picture and label the monster.
This allowed the pupils to re-read the text and elicit key pieces of information to enable them to do
this. As discussed above, this is a relatively low-level cognitive task but was engaging the pupils in
discussing the text and creating their monster.

It would be easy to skip over the first paragraph of this but Jake chose to direct the pupils to consider and collate as many bits of information as they could about the setting. He challenged them
to find as many different points as they could which encouraged the groups to re-read the paragraph and add more detail. His question here was: *How does this detail make you feel?* He asked
the children to note down their personal responses to this before they discussed it with their talk
partner. Here he was allowing a degree of freedom with the text and reminding them that having
a personal reaction to a text is a good start for any analysis as it gives greater credence to pupils'
ideas if they actually *felt* it.

As he moved on with the close reading, groups were asked to consider the following areas of the
text to explore:

- What words and phrases does Frankenstein use to describe his creation? The first one is
  'lifeless thing'. What do you think he is feeling towards his creation?
- Draw a line and note down Frankenstein's emotions during this extract. Begin with anxiety ('an
  anxiety that almost amounted to agony'). How does he feel by the end?
- Read from: *I started from my sleep* ... in paragraph 3. What does the monster do? What do you
  think he is trying to do? How does this make you feel? How did Frankenstein respond?

Pupils engaged with the structured talk although at one point Jake had to redirect the whole
class to the second area of exploration. He found that some groups needed him to model how to

(Continued)

(Continued)

approach this type of close reading as it was dealing with the extract as a whole. Another way to reinforce this was to ask two of his most able pupils if they could think of any reading tactics to approach this. One pupil discussed keeping the focus in their head, re-reading the task and skimming through the texts, underlining interesting/helpful phrases in pencil as they moved through the text. Having planned for these moments, he was able to hold on to the general atmosphere of engagement and interrogation of the text and the pupils re-focused.

Case study reflections

- How have you planned for close reading?
- What contingency plans do you use regularly to support pupils when required?
- How do you use questioning as a key part of teaching analysis?

The case study above illustrates how you can plan to teach close reading and introduce more challenging texts if this follows collaborative and exploratory work with the text first.

Moving children towards analysing texts with confidence

Pupil questioning and interrogation of text

Think about how your practice can develop as you move from teacher planned questions to *pupil* planned questions. After a first reading, can pupils create a set of questions that they would like to find an answer to or that they might pass on to another group? You can offer question stems to support them or explicitly share Bloom's Taxonomy (1956). Pennell (2014) found that with careful planning, dialogic learning environments and an awareness of pupils' experiential knowledge pupils were able to develop their critical awareness and analysis of texts. The building blocks from active approaches to reading through to collaborative working and exploratory talk create an environment where pupils can harness their cognitive ability. Once again, with a well-chosen text, pupils will clamour to interrogate the text as they have a vested interest in the plot and characters – they are intrigued to know how and why things happened.

Assessment

We have tentatively explored some of the means of assessing pupils' progress with analysis of texts throughout the commentary and case studies above. However, it is useful to extract some of these strategies and remind ourselves of the numerous opportunities to assess during active and collaborative lessons.

- *Pre-planned teacher questions* – this enables you to consider the cognitive demand and intricacy of the close reading in advance. By pitching these to pupils appropriately in order to develop stamina and offer scaffolded challenge, the teacher is able to respond to their answers accordingly. The differentiation here is twofold and allows an insight into the pupils' comprehension and ability to step back from the text.

- *Annotations* – guided annotations are an excellent way to build stamina and confidence with close reading and are quick and easy to assess during lesson time and afterwards. Two 'big questions' to consider for an extract and highlighters to show markings will give pupils a practical way into texts and a visual overview of their thoughts. This will lead easily into pair/share work or small group work to compare their findings. They then have their own scaffold for talk.

- *Teacher eavesdropping* – an intuitive and sensible way to assess progress during collaborative work. This allows the teacher to gauge pupils' engagement, comprehension and ability to analyse the text at the same time as picking up on misconceptions. Differentiation will occur as you intervene and challenge or support individual pupils or groups.

- *Written work* – the type of written response that you might lead into will be the point at which the above strategies will have cumulatively led the pupils towards a greater insight. However, there will be some pupils who will have shown a deep understanding of text, character motivations and authorial intent in collaborative or oral work but are less able to articulate this in the written form. The point at which you teach pupils how to convert this cognitive understanding into a written format is a point of consideration during the unit of work. Capturing thoughtful responses regularly in class and explicitly articulating how this might be written should be an ongoing part of the teacher commentary to bridge this gap between reading and writing.

CHAPTER SUMMARY

Within this chapter, we have explored how to promote curiosity around literature and how to do so within an environment of mutual trust, safety and engagement. The following provides a clear outline as to the strategic steps you might take in planning for close reading and analysis.

What?

Enable children to read with:

- Insight
- Inference
- Deduction
- Criticality

Why?

In order to build children's confidence with:

(Continued)

(Continued)

- Critical reading and understanding
  - ○ What did the author mean?
  - ○ How do we know?
  - ○ What language choices led us to this opinion?
  - ○ Do my peers agree?

How?

- Promote curiosity through well-chosen texts and active approaches to new texts
- Plan for collaborative approaches to learning
- Facilitate exploratory talk
- Develop teacher questioning
- Promote pupil questioning and interrogation of text
- Build on children's understanding of analysis by sharing processes

Further reading

Alexander, R (2004) *Towards Dialogic Teaching: rethinking classroom talk*. York: Dialogos UK.

Varga, A (2017) Metacognitive perspectives on the development of reading comprehension: A classroom study of literary text-talks, *Literacy, 51* (1) 19–25.

References

Alexander, R (2004) *Towards Dialogic Teaching: rethinking classroom talk*. York: Dialogos UK.

Austen, J (1994) *Northanger Abbey*. St Ives: Penguin Popular Classics.

Bloom, BS (1956) *Taxonomy of Educational Objectives: The classification of eduational goals, by a committee of college and university examiners. Handbook 1: Cognitive Domain*. New York: Longmans, Green.

Brett, A (2016) Seeking a balance: discussion strategies that foster reading with authorial empathy, *Journal of Adolescent and Adult Literacy, 60* (3): 295–304.

Brontë, E (1992) *Wuthering Heights*. Hertfordshire: Wordsworth Classics.

Brown, R (2008) The road not yet taken: A transactional strategies approach to comprehension instruction, *Reading Teacher, 61* (7): 538–47.

Brown, S and Kappes, L (2012) *Implementing the Common Core State Standards: A primer on 'close reading of text'*. Washington, DC: Aspen Institute, cited in D Fisher and N Frey (2014) Contingency teaching during close reading, *Reading Teacher, 68* (4): 277–86.

Clark, C and De Zoysa, S (2011) *Mapping the Interrelationships of Reading Enjoyment, Attitudes, Behaviour and Attainment: An exploratory investigation*. Leicester: National Literacy Trust.

Conan Doyle, A (1996) *The Hound of the Baskervilles*. London: Penguin Popular Classics.

Coultas, V (2016) Case studies of teachers' understandings of the pedagogy of classroom talk: Some critical moments explored, *Literacy, 50* (1): 32–9.

Department for Education (DfE) (2013) *The National Curriculum in England: Framework for Key Stages 1 to 4*. London: DfE.

Fisher, D and Frey, N (2014) Contingency teaching during close reading, *Reading Teacher, 68* (4): 277–86.

Horton, S, Beattie, L and Bingle, B (2015) *Lessons in Teaching Reading Comprehension in Primary School*. London: Sage/Learning Matters.

McGuinn, N (2014) *The English Teacher's Drama Handbook*. London: Routledge.

Mercer, N and Dawes, L (2008) The value of exploratory talk, in N Mercer and S Hodgkinson (eds) *Exploring Talk in School*. London: Sage.

Pennell, C (2014) In the age of analytic reading: Understanding readers' engagement with text, *Reading Teacher, 68* (4): 251–60.

Pressley, M (2000) What should comprehension instruction be the instruction of? In MI Kamil, PB Mosenthal, PD Pearson and R Barr (eds). *Handbook of Reading Research: Volume III*. New York: Lawrence Erlbaum.

Rojas-Drummond, S, Mazon, N, Littleton, K and Velez, M (2014) Developing reading comprehension through collaborative learning, *Journal of Research in Reading, 37* (2): 138–58.

Sachar, L (2000) *Holes*. London: Bloomsbury.

Shelley, M (2014) *Frankenstein*. New York: Millennium Publications.

Twist, L, Sizmur, J, Bartlett, S and Lynn, L (2012) *PIRLS 2011: Reading Achievement in England*. Slough: NFER.

6
QUESTIONING TEXTS

CHAPTER OBJECTIVES

This chapter will allow you to achieve the following outcomes:

- Have an awareness of the research associated with questioning to develop comprehension skills;
- Know how to plan for effective questioning;
- Understand different approaches to questioning a text.

LINKS TO THE TEACHERS' STANDARDS

Working through this chapter will help you meet the following standards:

1. Set high expectations which inspire, motivate and challenge pupils
2. Promote good progress and outcomes by pupils
3. Demonstrate good subject and curriculum knowledge
4. Plan and teach well-structured lessons
5. Adapt teaching to respond to the strengths and needs of all pupils

LINK TO THE NATIONAL CURRICULUM

Years 5 and 6 Programme of Study

Reading – comprehension

Pupils should be taught to:

- understand what they read by:
    - checking that the book makes sense to them, discussing their understanding and exploring the meaning of words in context
    - asking questions to improve their understanding
    - drawing inferences such as inferring characters' feelings, thoughts and motives from their actions, and justifying inferences with evidence
    - predicting what might happen from details stated and implied
    - summarising the main ideas drawn from more than one paragraph, identifying key details that support the main ideas
    - identifying how language, structure and presentation contribute to meaning
- discuss and evaluate how authors use language, including figurative language, considering the impact on the reader
- distinguish between statements of fact and opinion
- participate in discussions about books that are read to them and those they can read for themselves, building on their own and others' ideas and challenging views courteously
- explain and discuss their understanding of what they have read, including through formal presentations and debates, maintaining a focus on the topic and using notes where necessary
- provide reasoned justifications for their views.

(DfE, 2013)

The importance of questioning a text

Effective questioning can be used to encourage deeper thinking, reflection and evaluation and to challenge previously held assumptions. It is a powerful tool to use in the classroom and has its roots embedded in Greek philosophy – Socrates employed a number of questions to encourage his student to reflect critically upon his own thinking as outlined in Plato's *The Republic*.

Although Socratic questioning techniques may not be explicitly used in primary school classrooms, the principles underpin what is taking place. Children move forward in their learning when questions are used to extend thinking because they have opportunities to re-shape original ideas. At the same time, it allows teachers in the classroom to assess understanding and challenge learners to think more critically. Various critical thinking models and question taxonomies can be used to move children through the lower-level retrieval type questions towards the higher-order thinking skills that are characteristic of a 'good' reader. Deeper understanding occurs when children are asked higher order questions which foster metacognition (Baker and Brown, 1984; Fordham, 2006) and allows them to make links with prior knowledge and experiences. The role of questioning forms the backbone of classroom practice and is arguably most important when we consider developing reading comprehension.

As teachers, we are very aware of the difference between low-level questioning and questions that promote higher-order thinking skills. Research has shown that there is a high level of teacher talk in the classroom with teachers asking hundreds of questions a day (Brualdi, 1998; Alexander, 2004). Many of these are low-level questions which require factual answers based on retrieval or subject knowledge rather than used to invoke discussion and to challenge thinking (Alexander, 2004; Hattie, 2012). Hattie refers to the study conducted by Hardman *et al.* (2003) which stated that in 70 per cent of the time, the answers given usually consisted of less than three words or took less than five seconds to answer (Hattie, 2012). Of greater concern is the fact that children are often given only a few seconds thinking time before responding (Cazden, 2001). From this, it is clear to observe that teacher talk may dominate some classrooms, and more time needs to be devoted to facilitating discussion through questioning if we are to challenge readers. Alexander (2004) observes that when teachers use probing questions to encourage children themselves to develop questions, there is a positive effect on student engagement and learning. Through listening to children 'thinking aloud', teachers are able to determine levels of understanding and can challenge readers by intervening as appropriate.

When reading texts with children, whether individually, as a group or via whole-class teaching, there is a tendency to rely on text-dependent questions. These questions are perfectly acceptable in developing comprehension skills as they require the reader to use information in the text to inform opinion. Furthermore, we know that retrieval questions feature heavily in statutory tests, and while it is important that we use questioning to develop lifelong lovers of reading, we also have a duty to prepare children for Key Stage 1 and Key Stage 2 statutory assessments. However, using literal questions to move on to more challenging questions allows readers to *transcend the text and move beyond the meaning that the author presents* (Boele, 2016, p219). This allows children to form judgements about character, plot, setting and key themes as they evaluate what they have read and link it to their own prior knowledge and experiences. Rather than accepting what the author has to say, questions designed to interrogate meaning facilitate learning at greater depth as illustrated in the examples in Figure 6.1 which could be adapted to suit any text.

Othello – William Shakespeare	
Questions that transcend the text	**Questions about the text**
• How do the characters of Othello and Iago represent society today?	• How would you describe the characters of Othello and Iago?
• How does the author make us feel about Othello?	• How does the character of Othello change during the play?
• How does this play affect me and my beliefs?	• What are the key themes explored within this play?

Figure 6.1   Possible questions for deeper understanding

Higher-order questions demand analysis, evaluation and synthesis of ideas from both the text and beyond. When considering questions which transcend the text, pupils will need to argue, justify, negotiate and talk through their thought processes, leading to improved comprehension skills (Horton *et al.*, 2015).

Developing critical literacy

Pupils are required as part of the Key Stage 2 and Key Stage 3 curriculum to develop critical thinking skills by responding to a variety of texts. Reading comprehension is crucial in developing these skills as it provides a space for interpreting and discussing texts in light of prior knowledge, and encouraging readers to differentiate between fact and opinion. In addition, teaching children about inference, presentation and authorial voice enables them to reflect upon purpose and meaning in a more informed manner. But what do we mean by critical literacy and why is it so important?

RESEARCH FOCUS: CRITICAL LITERACY

There are multiple definitions of critical literacy which appear in the literature, although Lalik and Oliver state that there is a general consensus that a pedagogy for critical literacy is based on three tenets: literacy as a political consideration is linked to social justice and is transformative in its approach (Lalik and Oliver, 2007).

Key figures in the conceptualisation of this within the classroom are Freire and Macedo, whose work on reading texts to make sense of the world illustrates how our everyday experiences of the world around us influence our understanding of texts. This allows the reader to question knowledge and re-define it, leading to an altered perspective of the world: the word and the world being inextricably linked (Freire and Macedo, 1987).

According to Luke and Freebody, critical literacy involves the exploration of multiple perspectives whereby we consider the author's voice, the audience, the context and viewpoints that are not visible in order to derive meaning from the text (Luke and Freebody, 1997). Leland *et al.* explore this further as they believe that texts which raise social issues can make reading more relevant (Leland *et al.*, 2013), a key premise to our earlier chapter on using thematic approaches to develop comprehension skills.

The importance of critical literacy in understanding how texts are used to manipulate viewpoints and 'alter the world' (Luke, 2012, p9) is all too evident in today's society where there is a proliferation of 'fake news' which requires children to critically evaluate what they are reading. The National Literacy Trust has recently produced a report which explores the relationship between critical literacy and fake news, citing some interesting statistics:

A UK-based Ofcom survey in 2016 noted that 58% of 8- to 11-year-olds and 72% of 12- to 15-year-olds said they visited news sites or apps, and of these, just over one fifth believed all the information they found there to be true.

(Picton and Teravainen, 2017, p6)

Through critical literacy, we are able to support pupils in seeking alternative understandings and encourage them to question the perceived truth in order to re-define their view of the world. Thus it is imperative that we, as teachers, teach pupils to *read with and against the content, form and interests of the text in order to be able to redesign it* (Janks, 2012, p152).

Planning to use questions with higher-level readers

Questioning pupils on what they are reading is crucial for a number of reasons:

1. it facilitates assessment;

2. it develops deeper thinking;

3. it ascertains what the pupil knows about characters;

4. it allows pupils to talk through their ideas;

5. it facilitates an informed dialogue to extend meaning;

6. it allows pupils to situate their reading within a socio-cultural context;

7. it provides an opportunity to gather views about the text;

8. it informs future planning.

Bloom's taxonomy

In order to ensure that we have all of the opportunities above, planning questions into lessons is essential. There are a number of critical thinking models that can support the development of questioning and can be used to devise learning outcomes, success criteria and assessment opportunities. The original Bloom' s taxonomy (1956) clearly shows the hierarchy of questioning from knowledge through to evaluation and teachers are encouraged to use the higher levels of questioning to challenge children's thinking (Figure 6.2). Over time, there have been several different forms of the taxonomy, since it has been redefined to ensure it actively addresses the learning that takes place in today's classroom. In 2001, Anderson and Krathwohl revised Bloom's cognitive taxonomy, replacing nouns with verbs so as to more accurately represent knowledge and cognition (Anderson *et al.*, 2001). Figure 6.3 presents the updated version and it is this taxonomy that many teachers use to challenge higher-level readers through the use of questioning.

Barrett's taxonomy

Barrett's taxonomy of reading comprehension comprises five cognitive levels, each divided into between four and eight subcategories that relate specifically to understanding texts (Barrett, 1968). They differ in complexity, ranging from easy to difficult in terms of cognitive ability. The first two levels are literal comprehension and reorganisation which require pupils to focus on ideas and information that is explicitly presented in texts; they have to 'read the lines'. Inferential comprehension requires pupils to 'read between the lines' whereas the remaining two categories draw on pupils' ability to evaluate the text thus 'reading beyond the lines'. As such, it is clear to see that there is a hierarchical element to the model with the later categories demanding that pupils draw from their own experiences and backgrounds in order to make sense of the text. This will lead to the deeper level of discussion that we would wish to promote in the classroom through the use of open ended questions.

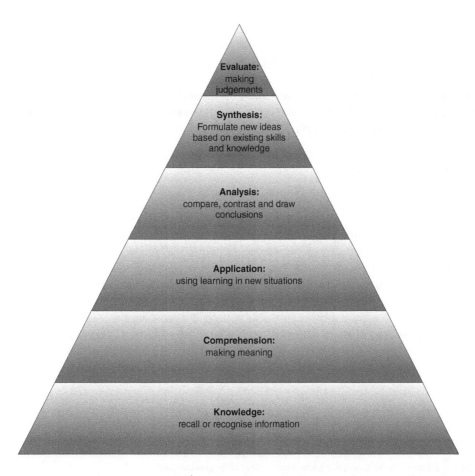

Figure 6.2   Bloom's taxonomy (based on a theoretical framework first presented in Bloom, 1956)

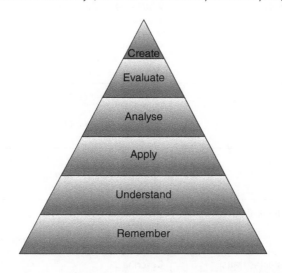

Figure 6.3   Revised Bloom's taxonomy (based on a revision by Anderson et al., 2001)

Planning questions based on Barrett's taxonomy is useful when engaging in discussion work around texts. If we are to challenge thinking and address the needs of higher level readers, it is important that texts are chosen wisely. There is a useful list of recommended texts in Chapter 3 which can be shared either as whole-class texts or group readers; once again, it may be worth stating that the criteria for texts to be challenging does not rely solely on the number of pages or the recommended age range for that book. Picture books and texts that are easily decodable are often just as challenging in terms of discussion, themes and deeper meanings.

Using Barrett's taxonomy

Table 6.1 outlines how the taxonomy can be used effectively to question pupils and generate discussion. It also references the content domains that are assessed in the Key Stage 2 tests so as to indicate opportunities for assessment. Question stems are useful to begin conversations and can be used with small groups when holding reading conferences or could be explored during whole class reading sessions whereby questions can be differentiated to ensure challenge for higher-level readers. This could be followed up by pupils writing their responses to individual questions and recording them to share with their peers and with teachers. The questions and activities below can be adapted to suit particular texts; it will require secure knowledge of individual texts by the teacher to ensure the use of significant questions. There are a number of websites listed at the end of this chapter that suggest texts that could be used to develop higher-level reading skills.

Table 6.1 *Planning questions based on Barrett's taxonomy*

Cognitive domains from Barrett's taxonomy			Questions/activities	Content domains
Literal comprehension	Recognition and recall	Details	Who? What? Where? Why? Tell me about ...	2b
		Main idea	What happened when or during ...? Show me where ...? Why did they do ...?	2b
		Sequence	What happened at the beginning/middle/end? What happened before/after ...? Retell the story.	2b, 2c
		Comparison	What are the differences between ...? How are these two characters different/similar?	2c
		Cause and effect	Why did this happen? What caused this? What reasons are given for going there?	2b
		Character traits	Describe ... How did he feel ...?	2a, 2b

Cognitive domains from Barrett's taxonomy		Questions/activities	Content domains
Reorganisation	Classifying	Which statements do not describe ...? Are there any puzzles?	2f
	Outlining	Create a story mountain.	2a
	Summarising	Retell the story to someone else.	2c
	Synthesising	What does this tell us about ... ?	2b
Inferential comprehension	Supporting details	Why do you think this happened?	2d
	Main ideas	What do you think led to this?	2d, 2h
	Sequence	What might happen next?	2e
	Comparisons	Compare the actions of ... with ...?	2d
	Cause and effect	What do you think will happen because of ...?	2e
	Character traits	What is the character's motive/purpose?	2d
	Outcomes	Predict what might have happened if ...?	2e, 2h
	Figurative language	What does this sentence/phrase/ metaphor mean? Why has the author used this?	2d, 2g
Evaluation	Judgements of reality or fantasy	Do you think this might happen?	2d, 2f
	Judgements of fact or opinion	Which version of events are true? How do you know?	2d, 2f, 2h
	Judgements of adequacy and validity	Is it acceptable to ...?	2f
	Judgements of appropriateness	How far do you agree with what he/she did?	2f
	Judgements of worth, desirability and acceptability	Is the character's attitude/behaviour/ action justifiable or acceptable? Why? Why not?	2f
Appreciation	Emotional response to the content	How did you respond to ...?	-
	Identification with characters or incidents	What might you have done in this situation?	-
	Reactions to the author's use of language	Discuss how effective the writer's use of language is when ...	2g
	Imagery	Can you hot seat? Act out your favourite scene from the story.	2d

Using pupils' questions

Question generation is a pedagogical tool for encouraging pupils to think a little more deeply about a text. It allows for deeper interrogation with a focus on a particular theme within the text. In the 2008 meta-analysis by Therrien and Hughes, they found that when pupils generated their own questions in response to a text, there were significant gains made in terms of reading comprehension (Therrien and Hughes, 2008). Furthermore, proficient readers ask more questions when engaging with a text which leads to further improvements in understanding (Ness, 2016), leading to a spiralling of critical thinking skills. By formulating their own questions, pupils can challenge assumptions within a text and contest information that is stated, arguably the skills of a higher-level reader.

When pupils are involved in constructing questions based on a text, they are more likely to become active participants in group discussions. They have a vested interest in the answers and greater motivation to find these through interacting with the text. Opportunities to discuss answers to these questions leads to active engagement which ultimately promotes a purposeful dialogue among participants (Lightner and Wilkinson, 2017; McKeown *et al.*, 2009).

Boele makes the point that *readers transcend the text when they question, challenge and evaluate the veracity of the author's message* (Boele, 2016, p217). So, what are the implications for classroom practice?

CASE STUDY

Tara had read *The Wolf Wilder* by Katherine Rundell as part of the 2017 UKLA book shadowing project (**https://ukla.org/awards/ukla-book-award**) and was keen to share it with her class as part of a whole-class read. She was aware that the book contained some rather challenging themes around war, loss, friendship and poverty and wanted to challenge children's thinking through discussion. Rather than set questions herself, she modelled how to develop their own questions by thinking aloud and talking though her reasons for each one. She then worked with her pupils to construct their own questions – before reading and immediately after each chapter – to be shared and discussed in small group reading conferences. This allowed her to concentrate on fluency, retrieval and inference questions during the class read.

Questions formulated for discussion by her class after reading Chapter 1:

- Why is the story set in Russia?
- How different would the opening have been if set in this country?
- Do the wolves really live in the house with Feodora?
- Is it right that the wolves are kept as pets? Do you think they were *untame*, as Feo insisted?
- Do you think the wolves killed the elk? Why? Why not?
- Is it right that the soldiers demanded compensation?
- How do you think the incident with the soldiers influenced what Feo would do?
- Are wolves 'vermin with teeth'?
- What kind of a person is Feo?

The questions were displayed on a working wall in the classroom and used to form the basis of small-group discussions which followed the class reading of the book. The answers to these questions could be found by actively engaging with the text which meant that there was a purposeful reason for reading the book. Having discussed initial questions, these were revisited following subsequent chapters and new questions were added to the wall to promote further discussion.

Further questions to encourage higher-order thinking can be found at: **www.tes.com/teaching-resource/the-wolf-wilder-by-katherine-rundell-teachers-notes-11107552**

Case study reflections

- Do you encourage pupils to formulate their own questions?
- Consider how you would facilitate small group discussion that leads to developing critical thinking.
- How might you assess children's understanding of the text based on pupils' question generation?

Questioning the author

We have explored how questioning a text can enhance readers' skills and develop critical thinking. It is important that we teach pupils to *comprehend* the text but, to develop higher-level thinking, we must model how to *interact* with the text. A useful pedagogy to employ is 'questioning the author' which not only allows pupils to seek more meaningful constructs, but also to question the status quo (Lightner and Wilkinson, 2017). This encourages a close reading of the text so that, once internalised, pupils will begin to automatically ask these questions. This can be done in a number of ways: through modelling questions, through the written interrogation of a text and through writing letters to authors as well as through tweeting authors to ask questions about their writing, hot seating children in role as the author and as part of small-group reading conferences where multiple viewpoints can be explored.

Questions drawn from the higher levels of Bloom's and Barrett's taxonomies can be used to model how to question the author. For example:

- What is the author trying to tell us?
- Do you think that the author is biased towards any of the characters? What makes you think that?
- How does the author make us feel about …?
- How does the author present that information? Why?
- Why do you think the author let us know about …?

- Do you think the author wants us to predict what happens? How does the author achieve this?

- Was the author right to suggest ...?

Encouraging children to use these questions while reading is crucial in developing higher-level readers who are able to critically reflect upon the meaning behind written text.

A question-friendly classroom

What makes a question-friendly classroom and why is this so important in our quest to engage and enthuse readers?

The way in which the teacher encourages and facilitates discussion around texts through questioning and modelling thought processes, together with acceptance of pupils' opinions, is a powerful process for developing a classroom ethos that develops higher-order thinking skills (Buchanan Hill, 2016). Open dialogue allows pupils to become more aware of issues and to develop empathy and creates a climate of acceptance and challenge (Lennon, 2017). Through careful management of this process, teachers are able to intervene as appropriate to further develop understanding within a 'safe' environment. To reflect upon your own classroom, consider the following:

- What percentage of teaching time is given over to pupil talk?

- How long do you give for pupils to respond?

- What strategies do you employ to facilitate thinking time?

- How do you organise small-group discussion?

- Do pupils ask you questions about the text?

- Do pupils feel 'safe' to convey their own opinions about themes explored in texts?

- How do you manage the flow of the discussion? Who contributes?

- Does your classroom environment allow for pupils to add questions to working walls?

Assessment

As previously stated, questioning is a crucial pedagogical tool for assessing understanding. However, we know that understanding is much more than simply regurgitating what has been read. It demands that the reader interacts with the text and the author in a meaningful manner so as to explore various critical perspectives. It requires skilful handling if we are to further develop comprehension skills and we will now explore ways in which we can use questioning to assess pupils' understanding.

- *Content domains.* Although content domains should not drive assessment or replace national curriculum coverage, they are useful to categorise questions. Use these to underpin the skills of comprehension while ensuring that your pupils are reading for pleasure and developing that lifelong love for books – they are, after all, skills that we would want children to develop in order to become proficient readers. The content domains categorise skills as in Table 6.2.

Table 6.2   Content domains

	Content domain	Useful questions stems
2a	Give/explain the meaning of words in context.	Why did the author choose this word? What does it tell us about … mood, character, atmosphere? How does this word/phrase make you feel? Why? Can you think of alternative words to use?
2b	Retrieve and record information/ identify key details from fiction and non-fiction	What happens? Where does … go? What was … like?
2c	Summarise main ideas from more than one paragraph	What are the key themes? Can you summarise the main points? Can you identify the non-essential information? Order the following points.
2d	Make inferences from the text/explain and justify inferences with evidence from the text	Why does … do this? Explain using examples from the text. How does … show … ? Is it fact or opinion? What makes you think that? Explain why …?
2e	Predict what might happen from details stated and implied	What might happen next? How do you know? Do you think … is possible? Why? What might be the outcome of this?
2f	Identify/explain how information/ narrative content is related and contributes to meaning as a whole	Can you suggest why … happened? How does this make us feel about …? Why do you think … acted in this way?
2g	Identify/explain how meaning is enhanced through choice of words and phrases	How has the author made you feel happy, sad, despondent, etc.? What does this description suggest about …?
2h	Make comparisons within the text	What are the similarities/differences? Compare these two events. How do the characters' moods compare?

(Based on the English Reading test framework, 2017)

- *Acronyms*. There are various acronyms that relate to specific skills; for example VIPERS which stands for Vocabulary, Inference, Prediction, Explanation, Retrieval, Summarise/sequence (**https://www.literacyshedblog.com/blog/reading-vipers**) or ERIC which encompasses Explain, Retrieve, Interpret, Choice (**https://misswilsonsays.wordpress.com/2016/10/09/free-eric-starters-to-support-reading-lessons/**). These are useful tools to focus questioning and ensure a breadth so as to assess effectively. Why don't you invent your own?

- *Assessing pupils' questioning skills*. Allow children time to formulate their own questions and record these either on sticky notes or on iPads so that you are able to survey the range of questions for individual pupils. This will allow you to target intervention appropriately.

CHAPTER SUMMARY

Within this chapter, we have explored the place of questioning as a pedagogical tool to further enhance comprehension skills and to foster a lifelong love for reading. By examining key research, we have situated the argument for using higher-level questioning to address the needs of skilful readers so as to enhance their critical thinking skills – a key component when exploring texts.

Further reading

Horton, S, Beattie, L and Bingle, B (2015) *Lessons in Teaching Reading Comprehension in Primary School*. London: Sage/Learning Matters.

Chapter 3 explores the use of questions with picture books to develop comprehension skills.

https://literacytrust.org.uk/resources/fake-news-and-critical-literacy/

An interesting exploration of the link between critical literacy and fake news.

https://www.booktrust.org.uk/books/

http://booksforkeeps.co.uk/

https://www.clpe.org.uk/corebooks/free-resources

These are all useful websites suggesting books that can be used in the classroom.

References

Alexander, R (2004) *Towards Dialogic Teaching: Rethinking classroom talk*. York: Dialogos UK.

Anderson, LW and Krathwohl, DR (eds) with Airasian, PW, Cruikshank, KA, Mayer, RE, Pintrich, PR, Raths, J and Wittrock, MC (2001) *A Taxonomy for Learning, Teaching, and Assessing: A revision of Bloom's Taxonomy of Educational Objectives (complete edition)*. New York: Longman.

Baker, L and Brown, AL (1984) Metacognitive skills and reading, in PD Pearson, R Barr, ML Kamil and P Mosenthal (eds) *Handbook of Reading Research*. New York: Longman.

Barrett, TC (1968) Taxonomy of cognitive and affective dimensions of reading comprehension, in T. Clymer (ed.) *What is 'Reading'? Some current concepts*. Chicago: University of Chicago Press.

Bloom, BS (1956) *Taxonomy of Educational Objectives: the classification of educational goals, by a committee of college and university examiners. Handbook I: Cognitive Domain*. New York: Longmans, Green.

Boele, A (2016) Text-dependent questions: Reflecting and transcending the text, *Reading Teacher, 70* (2): 217–20.

Brualdi Timmins, A (1998) Classroom questions. *Practical Assessment, Research and Evaluation, 6* (6). Available online: **http://PAREonline.net/getvn.asp?v=6&n=6**

Buchanan Hill, J (2016) Questioning techniques: A study of instructional practice. *Peabody Journal of Education, 91* (5) 660–671.

Cazden, CB (2001) *Classroom Discourse: The language of teaching and learning*, 2nd edition. Portsmouth: Heinemann.

Department for Education (DfE) (2013) *The National Curriculum in England: Framework for Key Stages 1 to 4*. London: DfE.

Fordham, N (2006) Crafting questions that address comprehension strategies in content reading, *Journal of Adolescent and Adult Literacy, 49* (5): 390–6.

Freire, P and Macedo, D (1987) *Literacy: Reading the word and the world*. New York: Routledge.

Hattie, J (2012) *Visible Learning for Teachers: Maximizing impact on learning*. Oxford: Routledge.

Horton, S, Beattie, L and Bingle, B (2015) *Lessons in Teaching Reading Comprehension in Primary School*. London, Sage/Learning Matters.

Janks, H (2012) The importance of critical literacy, *English Teaching, 11* (1): 150–63.

Lalik, R and Oliver, KL (2007) Differences and tensions in implementing a pedagogy of critical literacy with adolescent girls, *Reading Research Quarterly, 42* (1): 46–70.

Leland, C, Lewison, M and Harste, JC (2013) *Teaching Children's Literature: It's critical!* New York: Routledge.

Lennon, S (2017) Questioning for controversial and critical thinking dialogues in the social studies classroom, *Issues in Teacher Education, 26* (1): 3.

Lightner, S and Wilkinson, IAG (2017) Instructional frameworks for quality talk about text: Choosing the best approach, *Reading Teacher, 70* (4): 435–43.

Luke, A (2012) Critical literacy: Foundational notes, *Theory Into Practice, 51* (1): 4–11.

Luke, A and Freebody, P (1997) The social practices of reading, in S Muspratt, A Luke and P Freebody (eds) *Constructing Critical Literacies: Teaching and learning textual practice*. Cresskill, NJ: Hampton Press.

McKeown, MG, Beck, IL and Blake, RGK (2009) Rethinking reading comprehension instruction: A comparison of instruction for strategies and content approaches, *Reading Research Quarterly, 44* (3): 218–53.

Ness, M (2016) When readers ask questions: Inquiry-based reading instruction, *Reading Teacher, 70* (2): 189–96.

Picton, I and Teravainen, A (2017) *Fake News and Critical Literacy: An evidence review*. London: National Literacy Trust.

Rundell, K (2015) *The Wolf Wilder*. London: Bloomsbury.

Therrien, W and Hughes, C (2008) Comparison of repeated reading and question generation on students' reading fluency and comprehension, *Learning Disabilities, 6* (1): 1–16.

7
INTERTEXTUALITY

(Continued)

- maintain positive attitudes to reading and understanding of what they read by:
  - continuing to read and discuss an increasingly wide range of fiction, poetry, plays, non-fiction and reference books or textbooks
  - identifying and discussing themes and conventions in and across a wide range of writing
  - making comparisons within and across books
- understand what they read by:
  - checking that the book makes sense to them, discussing their understanding and exploring the meaning of words in context
  - asking questions to improve their understanding
  - drawing inferences such as inferring characters' feelings, thoughts and motives from their actions, and justifying inferences with evidence
  - identifying how language, structure and presentation contribute to meaning
- discuss and evaluate how authors use language, including figurative language, considering the impact on the reader
- participate in discussions about books that are read to them and those they can read for themselves, building on their own and others' ideas and challenging views courteously
- explain and discuss their understanding of what they have read, including through formal presentations and debates, maintaining a focus on the topic and using notes where necessary
- provide reasoned justifications for their views.

(DfE, 2013)

What do we mean by intertextuality?

We have considered how effective planning of reading and response to texts can encourage children to become active participants in their own comprehension and understanding. We have also explored the ways in which active approaches and peer learning can support this. Referring back to the Programme of Study for KS2 (DfE, 2013), we should consider how this pedagogy now leads us to promote the positive approaches to reading: *identifying and discussing themes and conventions in and across a wide range of writing and making comparisons within and across books* (DfE, 2013).

Consideration of the connectedness of texts leads us to teaching pupils about comparison and intertextuality. All readers will inevitably bring to the text their previous experiences of text, the connections with life as a whole and relationships therein (Latham, 2008). Young children intuitively understand intertextuality as they make sense of the world and their first experience of reading books as picture books. Evans' *speculative ponderings* (2016) unlocks this process for children as the open questions allow them to draw upon their previous experiences of ideas, themes, words and phrases. It is the development of this process through comparison and the opportunity to make links between texts which will promote greater critical thinking and therefore deepen the understanding of more challenging texts.

CASE STUDY: PLANNING FOR LEARNING THROUGH INTERTEXTUALITY

This case study explores how a teacher's planning resulted in:

1. an increase in pupils' curiosity towards texts and themes;
2. better understanding of *how* to make links and connections;
3. more elaborate responses to open questions.

Stacey was interested in developing the comparison skills in her Year 6 class following a continuing professional development day which had examined how KS2 teachers could extend the reading skills of pupils. She had been particularly attracted to the idea of planning in more of a range of texts to allow the pupils to make connections and therefore build their interpretive skills. It had also appealed to her creative nature when putting together units of work.

She was keen to think about the connections between texts in terms of comparing texts written at a similar time and at a different time and the associated themes between them. She opted to choose a seemingly simplistic idea which would connect all of the texts and interest her learners: 'the haunted house'. From here, she thought carefully about how she could inject challenge through the texts she chose, the contrast of the different eras in which they were written (and therefore, implicitly, the intended reader) and how the theme might vary.

Stacey wanted to build up the pupils' stamina for dealing with a range of texts, but was also clear that she needed to establish basic comparative skills at the outset. To that end, while she had a good overview of the texts she would be working with, she wanted to ensure that she could model and then scaffold a close reading and comparison of two texts. She decided to start with an extract from *Wuthering Heights* (Emily Brontë, 1992) and *Jane Eyre* (Charlotte Brontë, 1992), which focused on the setting of the gothic nature of the house and the pervading sense of gloom. Having carefully edited the text to ensure that the pupils would be dealing with extracts which focused on setting and tone, Stacey then planned some of the questions which would scaffold group talk to make sense of the text. She thought through the best way to home in on aspects of the text which would be encouraging a close reading and also beginning to prompt comparison and contrasts between the two (*Wuthering Heights*, pp2-3; *Jane Eyre*, pp112-13 and pp124-5).

As she had chosen challenging texts from a similar time period, the pupils would be in an equal mindset when dealing with the more archaic nature of the language. Scaffolding with glossary terms as appropriate to the different children's needs would support them with any difficulties here. She felt that this choice of dual texts would lead more naturally to a consideration of the tone and 'feel' of the text rather the pupils comparing texts from different centuries at this stage.

Having read the extracts to the pupils, Stacey began with some basic directed activities related to texts (DARTs) to engage them with the detail of the language. The pupils scanned the printed extracts and highlighted key words which contributed to the description of Thornfield and Wuthering Heights and this allowed them to extract a range of vocabulary and consider the impact of these word choices on the reader. She then set up the groups for collaborative work and moved

(Continued)

(Continued)

the pupils towards the questions which focused on the setting. Questions encouraged a personal response to the texts as the pupils worked in groups:

- *What impressions do you have of the weather at Wuthering Heights?*
- *How would you feel walking through the front door here and looking at the carvings?*
- *How would it feel to be standing in the 'family sitting room' and can you explain your answer?*
- *How would Jane feel as she was shown to her bedroom on her first night at Thornfield Hall?*
- *How does her reaction confirm this as she enters her bedroom and shuts the door?*
- *How did you react when you read about the laughter coming from the attic? What atmosphere does this create?*
- *Why do you think Brontë mentioned that it was daylight when Jane first heard the laugh?*

Stacey then provided the groups with sheets of A3 paper in different colours to try and organise some of their thoughts and responses to these two texts (a graphic organiser would work equally here). She designated roles at this point to ensure that there was a sense of purpose and momentum to this part of the collaborative talk where she wanted pupils to consider their array of ideas and classify them into different groups. She kept the classification simple at this point and asked them where there were similarities in tone, description or setting and where there were differences.

She found that the layered scaffolding had helped the pupils in being able to synthesise their group reading and analysis. The step-by-step approach had also allowed her to document the process of the reading through her teacher commentary and through her high expectations at each stage of the learning. Well-chosen groups of pupils enabled Stacey to challenge some of the more able pupils to take on the role of managing the talk to ensure that the collation of ideas had some direction. Two of the groups needed extra support at this point and Stacey was able to intervene and show how the organisation of their ideas on paper would make their group talk clearer.

Case study reflections

- How do you plan for the inclusion of a range of texts in units of work?
- In what ways do planned activities enhance pupils' ability to make connections and compare?
- What might pupils say about how they manage thinking about more than one text?

The importance of intertextuality in the reading journey

The inclusion of intertextuality in the reading process will have a significant impact on the pupils' ability to make connections between real world experiences and text based experiences. The ability to cope with such cognitive processes will build their reading stamina and their confidence as they inevitably deal with an increasing range of texts as they move into the higher Key Stages, both in English and other curricula subjects (Schmit, 2013).

A teacher's understanding of this significance is imperative if planning and teaching is to incorporate intertextuality as a concept to promote progress in reading ability. The pupils will build their interpretive skills through such comparisons and therefore have more freedom of thought when trying to make meaning (Shonoda, 2012). There are so many ways in which this can be a creative inclusion in the curriculum: comparisons between texts, of the same text but in different modes and links to contextual aspects of a text.

RESEARCH FOCUS: UNDERSTANDING INTERTEXTUAL MEANING-MAKING

In many teachers' planning sessions, there is the forethought to include active approaches to texts to keep the pupils engaged and curious, while recognising that this will also be supporting the process of comprehension. Understanding the importance of collaborative meaning-making has been explored in Chapter 5. This continues through to our consideration of intertextuality as a concept within reading. Barthes' model of intertextual interpretation suggested that the reader moves in and out of the range of texts in order to create connections (1976).

However, Shonoda (2012) has gone on to enquire how the different cognitive processes used in these instances are different to those in a linear text or sole text, so that we can further our understanding of how the children are thinking and learning to think as they engage in activities around comparing. She goes on to suggest that there is a certain playfulness associated with the way that the young reader has to 'fill in the gaps' as they manage their understanding of the primary text and the intertext.

Her work went on to highlight how the cognitive processes used in intertextual considerations are similar to those used when decoding metaphoric expression (Shonoda, 2012). For all teachers of literacy, this will make both the challenges and the benefits clear for pupils' understanding of text. It also brings into the realm of such planning a reminder that activities with younger children, such as retellings and, later, adaptations, are also sustained types of intertextuality (Shonoda, 2012, and Siegel, 1995, in Schmit, 2013).

Latham (2008) exemplified the power of intertextuality as he explored the overt use of this in David Almond's novel, *Skellig* (1998), and the impact that this had on empowering adolescent readers. He noted that there were different layers of intertextuality both in consideration of the relationships which were evident, the emotions therein and the inclusion of literary references to delve into but which wouldn't detract from the ongoing narrative. The inclusion of Blake's poetry is an addition rather than a diversion and opens up a multitude of teaching and reading opportunities. To that end, such explicit intertextuality gave an acknowledged respect to his young readers as they were encouraged to reflect on this sense of variety and the interrelationships between them. Latham describes the readers as *active participants* in the making of meaning as they are absorbed into the novel (2008).

CASE STUDY: LAYERING MEANING AND MAKING CONNECTIONS THROUGH INTERTEXTUALITY

As Stacey elicited pupils' thoughts about the two texts through the previous activity, she was able to build their confidence and noted that some of her more reticent pupils were better able to contribute to the whole-class discussion. She spent some time moving their personal but interpretive responses into some drama work where they had the opportunity to role play being Mr Lockwood standing in Wuthering Heights for the first time, or being Jane, walking down the corridor from the attic and hearing the strange laughter permeating the hallway. Having planned initial responses to the texts, the pupils were able to confidently express opinions and adopt thought-provoking commentaries to the settings they imagined.

The right choice of texts and sense of intrigue had hooked her pupils into the theme of gothic settings and the foreboding tone. She introduced the pupils to the names of the writers and gave them a little background on their familial links before suggesting that they read some different texts which would give them additional information about these two female writers in the nineteenth century. Having done the research in advance, she provided extracts from non-fiction texts which added to the background information of the women, their life on the Yorkshire moors, the Parsonage at Howarth and the pseudonyms that they adopted in order to be published writers. The children were intrigued to know more about them, in particular their home and social life. Stacey carefully constructed some activities around non-fiction texts which gave the pupils the opportunity to extract information which helped them to 'make sense of' the classification work they had previously done on the settings of the two novels. In their groups she suggested that they develop a 'mood board' which they could create to show the links between segments of text and the Brontës' lives.

The pupils were excited by the creative freedom that they were being given and were able to use the carefully scaffolded reading 'props' that they had been exposed to. Stacey was impressed to see how committed they were to creating their own group mood board and was delighted to see that many pupils were intuitively commenting on language choice, implicit reader inferences and the real-life context of the sisters' solitary life on the moors. The less able pupils had been provided with extracts which had colour-coded suggestions of words or phrases which they could home in on to enable them to begin the close reading without worrying about the scanning stage of this reading activity.

The final creative work was shown to the head teacher and commended at the weekly assembly for its contribution to the school ethos for reading. At this point Stacey was able to introduce an independent writing task based on this work. The written responses showed that the scaffolded intertextual work had worked as a longer-term scaffold, reducing the need for sentence prompts or writing frames for the less able. Stacey sensed that the pupils were invested in the reading and their own understanding of the connections and differences and had written enthusiastically and with depth as a result.

Case study reflections

- How do you plan for a range of intertext opportunities?
- How do you scaffold the learning to give pupils greater confidence with finding and managing connections between texts?
- What do you consider to be the benefits of introducing intertextuality to the meaning-making process in reading?

Types of intertextuality

We have seen from the varied perspectives of the case studies thus far that there are different ways of viewing intertextuality when planning for literacy units of work. Planning and teaching intertextually is a complex and challenging process (Ciecierski, 2017) so it is important from the process at the outset to consider the most appropriate model for our learners. Hartman and Allison (1996) suggested that there were four models for us to consider when incorporating intertextuality into literacy learning.

The four models were companion texts, corresponding texts, contradictory texts and cluster texts. Companion texts assume a commonality between texts which then allows for a consideration of variations between them. A corresponding text (popular within literacy teaching) would be connected by theme and allows the pupils to delve more deeply into a text by considering it in light of the linked text. A contradictory text is suggested as one which will provide multiple perspectives on a specific topic and a cluster text will provide the pupils with the surrounding texts which add to or connect to the initial text (Hartman and Allison, 1996).

In the case studies above, the *Wuthering Heights* and *Jane Eyre* extracts might be considered to be companion texts. The non-fiction texts about the Brontë sisters could be described as cluster texts. The importance of purpose is paramount at the planning stage. If pupils have considered texts previously in an isolated manner then there needs to be a rationale behind the intertextual approach – what is the learning intention? Once this has been pinpointed and the learning plans pitched to the learners, then there will be opportunity for deeper consideration of texts (Ciecierski, 2017).

CASE STUDY

As Stacey moved further into the unit of work she was keen to expand the breadth of literature around the theme of the haunted house. Having challenged the pupils with some nineteenth-century literature she was keen to build on this to increase the reading stamina and also to introduce some twentieth-century text to inject some comparative perspectives. To that end, she used an extract from *Rebecca*, when the new Mrs de Winter arrives at Manderley. The comparison between *Jane Eyre* and *Rebecca* is common-place in a literary sense but for pupils of this age range would be interesting for her class to explore.

She re-read the opening to the novel and decided that she would focus on quality over quantity of text and therefore chose the first three paragraphs. The description goes on with vivid and colourful clarity, but she did not want to overwhelm her pupils with a dense text. To that end, following a teacher reading, she read the text for a second time and asked the pupils to undertake a visualisation activity on plain paper. As well as using symbols or sketches, pupils were allowed to write down key words which stood out to them as they listened. They then had some pair/share time when they looked at each other's sketches and explained them. The big question posed to the class at this point was, 'what other text does this remind you of?' Again, this was followed by time to think and talk before Stacey led into a feedback session.

(Continued)

(Continued)

Stacey was able to elicit different ideas from the class, many of which included responses which noted the similarity in tone and mood to both *Jane Eyre* and *Wuthering Heights*. Some pupils also began to interject with references to other gothic reading, including more contemporary fiction. Stacey was pleased to note that they were making connections based on theme and tone but some of the more able pupils were also beginning to layer in how the authors had handled these differently. Her homework that week was targeted to varying abilities and tied in with wider reading for these able pupils. They were asked to prepare a review of a book of their choice which included connections or comparisons with any of the three extracts that they had studied so far. Those pupils who had not read any contemporary gothic literature were given an extract from *Goth Girl and the Ghost of a Mouse* (Riddell, 2013) or *Dial-a-Ghost* (Ibbotson, 1996) to consider. Two pupils opted to read the text as a whole and the librarian had copies on hold after discussions with Stacey some weeks before. In this sense, these pupils would be able to consider the texts as companions (Hartman and Allison, 1996) where there is a 'common axis' but variations in techniques or handling of the gothic nature.

Case study reflections

- In what way do you promote the cognitive challenge of considering varied texts to find connections and comparisons?
- How do you consider the added challenge for more able pupils when considering intertextual study?

The case study above illustrates how time spent planning effective text choices and thoughtful connections with other texts can promote both breadth and depth of reading interpretations.

Moving children towards an implicit understanding of the power of intertextuality

Intertextuality as part of analytical response

The planning process necessitates that teachers have a clear purpose and intended learning outcomes for their pupils when they are developing analytical responses. To that end, there are a variety of learning strategies which teachers will choose to complement this purpose and outcome. This might be developing pupils' inference skills through 'detective work' as they move towards reading between the lines or using a graphic organiser to collate their thoughts and make sense of patterns. In the same way, introducing a range of well-chosen texts will not only build reading stamina but also heighten the cognitive value of the analysis by asking pupils to think laterally, to find connections, to find differences and to evaluate the impact from the reader's point of view. This process enhances not only analytical reading but also interpretive reading.

The inclusion of school librarians or teaching assistants who are involved with the reading for pleasure programme should also be planned for. The types of reading that pupils are involved with can be varied and complex. Librarians are well-placed to help individuals or groups of pupils to navigate these interactions with texts so that they become familiar and confident in taking risks with literature (Schmit, 2013). This also promotes the view that they can have a personal response and that this is valued within any connections that they make.

Through the encouragement of transmediation, pupils are also likely to see that they deal with such connections when they step in and out of different modes, for example reading a book and then seeing the film or vice versa. The inclusion of moving image/film in the process of meaning-making can be powerful for pupils to see patterns and themes on different levels. They are adept at managing the different sign systems in society and so this should be a natural and integral part of our literacy teaching (Schmit, 2013; Clyde, 2003).

Assessment

When reading the case studies above, you will have noted that there were several opportunities for the teacher to assess pupils' progress. We will extract some of these for specific consideration here.

- *Questions for class discussions*. While some questions will intuitively build towards a deeper exploration of text, perhaps using Bloom's taxonomy as a structure would be useful. Some questions will need to be pre-planned if they are to truly challenge interpretation and analysis. As previously explored, the teacher's grasp of analysis and ability to feedback flexibly can build on pupils' skills as they discuss aspects of text. Likewise, it will point to gaps in understanding for the teacher to address.

- *Giving feedback on the mood board*. While this will be seen as low stakes from the pupils' point of view, the assessment of understanding at this point will be substantial. It is an ideal opportunity to intervene with certain groups of pupils and differentiate at the point of need through spontaneous questioning.

- *Listening to pupils' discussions about their visualisations*. This is low-stakes assessment for pupils if time and effort has been spent creating a safe environment. At this point the teacher can not only see how the pupils have interpreted key words and phrases in the text but also hear how they articulate this to their peers in their explanations.

- *Written work*. Specifically this refers to Stacey's written task comparing the two extracts at the start of this process. However, this can also take the form of a variety of more formal tasks or assessments and be structured around a definite comparison between texts. Equally, there are many opportunities through creative writing where pupils have to imagine that they are a character from the text. This might be a springboard from some of the character questions in the case studies above where pupils consider how Jane or Lockwood felt when they first entered these buildings.

CHAPTER SUMMARY

During this chapter we have considered what intertextuality means within the primary classroom and the value of encouraging this within literacy lessons. As well as defining the term for the teacher, we have had the opportunity to reflect on some case studies which highlight the inclusion of intertextual strategies to promote deeper reading responses.

Further reading

Allen, G (2011) *Intertextuality*. London: Routledge.

A useful overview of intertextuality within the realms of literary theory.

Barthes, R (1981) Theory of the text, in R Young (ed.) *Untying the Text*. London: Routledge, pp31–47.

Some of Roland Barthes' theories that underpin much of the work around intertextuality.

Serafini, F (2015) The appropriation of fine art into contemporary narrative picturebooks, *Children's Literature in Education, 46*: 438–53.

References

Almond, D (1998) *Skellig*. Hodder: London.

Barthes, R (1976) *The Pleasure of the Text*, trans. Richard Miller. London: Cape.

Brontë, C (1992) *Jane Eyre*. Hertfordshire: Wordsworth Classics.

Brontë, E (1992) *Wuthering Heights*. Hertfordshire: Wordsworth Classics.

Ciecierski, L (2017) What the common core state standards do not tell you about connecting texts, in *Reading Teacher, 71* (3): 285–94.

Clyde, J (2003) Stepping inside the story world: The subtext strategy – a tool for connecting and comprehending, *Reading Teacher, 57* (2): 150–9.

Department for Education (DfE) (2013) *The National Curriculum in England: Framework for Key Stages 1 to 4*. London: DfE.

du Mautier, D (2003) *Rebecca*. London: Virago Press.

Evans, J (2016) Who am I? Why am I here? and Where do I come from? Responding to philosophical picturebooks, *Education 3–13, 44* (1): 53–67.

Hartman, D and Allison, J (1996) Promoting inquiry-oriented discussions using multiple texts, in L Gambrell and J Almasi (eds) *Lively Discussions! Fostering engaged reading*. Newark, DE: International Reading Association, pp106–33.

Ibbotson, E (1996) *Dial-a-ghost*. London: Macmillan Children's Books.

Latham, D (2008) Empowering adolescent readers: Intertextuality in three novels by David Almond, *Children's Literature in Education, 39*: 213–26.

Riddell, C (2013) *Goth Girl and the Ghost of a Mouse*. Basingstoke: Pan Macmillan.

Schmit, K (2013) Making the connection: Transmediation and children's literature in library settings, *New Review of Children's Literature and Librarianship, 19* (1): 33–46.

Shonoda, M (2012) Metaphor and intertextuality: A cognitive approach to intertextual meaning-making in metafictional fantasy novels, *International Research in Children's Literature, 5* (1): 81–96.

8
INTERPRETATION OF TEXTS

- understand what they read by:
  - checking that the book makes sense to them, discussing their understanding and exploring the meaning of words in context
  - asking questions to improve their understanding
  - drawing inferences such as inferring characters' feelings, thoughts and motives from their actions, and justifying inferences with evidence
  - predicting what might happen from details stated and implied
  - summarising the main ideas drawn from more than one paragraph, identifying key details that support the main ideas
  - identifying how language, structure and presentation contribute to meaning
- discuss and evaluate how authors use language, including figurative language, considering the impact on the reader
- participate in discussions about books that are read to them and those they can read for themselves, building on their own and others' ideas and challenging views courteously
- explain and discuss their understanding of what they have read, including through formal presentations and debates, maintaining a focus on the topic and using notes where necessary
- provide reasoned justifications for their views.

(DfE, 2013)

What do we mean by interpreting texts?

Having considered how we build pupils' skills in analysing and questioning a text, we should now consider how pupils can apply their understanding to create their own interpretation. In so doing, they will be taking some autonomy of their view of the text and will need to consider how they react to different views. To be able to interpret a text we have to be able to make sense of it. This will include ordering our understanding of the concrete elements of the text and managing any abstract concepts (Levine, 2014). The juggling of these skills requires children to undertake literary reasoning. Levine (2014) goes on to explain how novice readers will need to draw on the context of the text and any personal knowledge they can bring to the fore to help them to do this. If the teacher draws attention to this and explains the process, they can reflect on the process and what they understand, thereby moving from a literal reading to interpretive sense-making.

Levine's research monitored the progress of pupils who were taken through everyday affect-based decisions as an explicit process to show them how they already interpreted the world on a daily basis. One such activity was talking about song lyrics which showed that they interpreted what they heard in order to ascribe meaning to the song. Throughout this process, the teacher is modelling how we think to interpret and encouraging a meta-cognition which can then be applied elsewhere as a transferable skill.

CASE STUDY: PLANNING TO TEACH INTERPRETATION SKILLS

This case study explores how a teacher's planning resulted in:

1. an increase in pupils' confidence when expressing an opinion;
2. closer engagement with and empathy towards characters;
3. more thoughtful responses to the text as a whole.

Manisha planned to read *Kensuke's Kingdom* by Michael Morpurgo with her Year 6 class. She felt that this would be an appropriate choice of text due to the dramatic disappearance of the main character, Michael, and the sense of adventure as he manages to survive and live on a desert island for a year. She was particularly interested in the tensions in family relations when Michael's parents lost their jobs in a local industry. As the story progressed, she thought that Michael's handling of his survival on the island would be interesting to explore, especially as he had to negotiate his presence there with another, older inhabitant, Kensuke.

Manisha mapped out the opportunities for group discussion and drama across the scheme of work and chunked the novel according to the most dramatic or tense parts of the plot. This allowed her to extract key themes and link them to everyday feelings and a real-world context for the pupils, such as loneliness or fear. One such example was exploring the tensions in the family during Chapter 1 when Michael learns that his father has left in search of a new job. Manisha structured a group activity which allowed pupils to read about Michael's mother's reaction to this and how she explained this to him. Pupils revisited the extract and underlined words which might imply a particular feeling; such as anger, annoyance or frustration for the mother, or confusion, sadness or worry for Michael. Certain groups were supported with some sentences underlined to direct them to the right parts of the text. This allowed them to access the cognitive part of the activity in an inclusive way.

She then asked them to discuss their reactions to the words they had underlined and to explain why the author had used these words: what was Morpurgo trying to get the reader to think or feel? In this way she was building on the analytical work that they had undertaken beforehand when they were examining the author's craft. The difference with moving towards an interpretive approach was that she then set up some drama activities which would allow them to explore the characters' feelings in more detail. She asked for volunteers for the mother and Michael to be sculpted into position at the moment when Michael finally learns that his father has left. Manisha had a copy of the extract on the whiteboard and pupils could refer to a paper copy too. The room had been organised to free up as much space as possible and tables were stacked around the side. As pupils were giving their suggestions for how the two characters should stand (still) and their stance, Manisha was regularly asking them to explain why they thought this. In doing so, she was cultivating an informal and safe environment in which the pupils were beginning to interpret text. Manisha was able to use her teacher commentary to articulate this process to the pupils so that they could see how they had taken a word from a written text and made their own interpretation. She was also able to demonstrate how there might be more than one interpretation of a word as pupils suggested different positions for the pupils being sculpted. The commentary allowed her to build a meta-language around the reading of the text which she would be able to build on later.

Case study reflections

- How do you plan for active approaches to texts in order to build foundations for interpretation skills?
- In what ways does teacher commentary feature in this and enhance the learning experience?
- What might pupils say about there being more than one 'right' answer?

The importance of interpreting texts

Young readers need to be reassured that they may have different views of the messages within a text. As we are teaching them to delve deeply into texts and understand how the writer has crafted language, we are also guiding them towards having a personal response to texts. At times, this will be intuitive and a natural part of the reading process as they draw on their own world experiences in order to make sense of what they are reading. At other times, they will need this process to be scaffolded so that they can see how their current knowledge and understanding of the world can help them to build a response. They may start to see this as problem-solving as they embark upon literary interpretation (Lee *et al.*, 2016).

In acknowledging the difficulties that pupils can have when trying to interpret texts, teachers will need to recognise the significance of building this skill in an explicit fashion at the planning stage. As teachers, our planning needs to ensure that pupils have the opportunity to go beyond the literal, to use inference to engage more deeply with text and to have a personal or emotional response to a literary text (Sosa *et al.*, 2016).

RESEARCH FOCUS: INTERPRETATION AND EXPERIENCE

When teaching analysis of texts, teachers need to ensure that the process of decoding the literary devices used does not deter children from having an emotional response to text. It is the ability to do the latter which provides children with the means to move into an interpretive mode. Research suggests that as analysis has become the forefront of pedagogical approaches to teaching literature, pupils have become disconnected from what they are reading (Eva-Wood, 2004). It is possible to step back from a text and view it with an air of objectivity in order to deconstruct the technical ways in which the text was put together. Therefore pupils can become adept at observing the writer's craft and formulating a critique. However, this level of analysis can detract from an engagement with the language, its nuances and making personal observations (Eva-Wood, 2004).

Eva-Wood (2004) suggests that as educators we need to be aware of the tension between the mechanics of reading and the experience of reading. At the heart of most schools, the importance of reading for pleasure is understood and there is a range of ways in which teachers mitigate

(Continued)

(Continued)

the absence of books in the home or a place to enjoy a book both emotionally and cognitively. Likewise, the link between reading for pleasure and attainment is well documented in research and the media. However, it is the explicit acknowledgement of the link between the *experience* of reading and the ability to interpret that can be fostered further.

Fialho *et al.* (2011) went on to research how tasks that explicitly required students to reason about a text affectively would promote deeper, more thoughtful responses to text while still incorporating analysis. Questions which encouraged a focus on an emotional connection with or exploration of characters and their actions, drew out responses as part of an experiential approach. Eva-Wood (2004) explored how experts and novices approached reading. In order to build the stamina of novice readers, she discovered that an emotional response to poetry would affect both understanding and interpretation. To that end, she suggested that if emotions can play a role in understanding stylistic devices and interpretation, then a more explicit discussion of emotion should take place in the classroom.

CASE STUDY: USING DRAMA TO ELICIT AN EMOTIONAL RESPONSE TO LITERATURE

Returning to Manisha's classroom experience of *Kensuke's Kingdom*, we will now explore some of the explicit ways in which she used drama strategies as active approaches to the text in order to develop greater empathy for characters and support children when making interpretations.

After the class had sculpted two children into position for the point at which Michael discovers his father had left, Manish asked the pupils to talk to their partners about how they thought the mother was feeling at this point. She also asked them to think about Michael's reaction and to use their underlined words to help them to construct meaning in their pairs. This way she had planned in rehearsal time for what was about to become a larger class discussion through drama.

After three minutes she stopped the pupils' talk and asked them to use their ideas to think about what either of the two characters might say at this point in the text. After two minutes she stopped them again. She had eavesdropped on some of the discussions and heard two thoughtful responses. She asked these two pupils if they would stand next to the sculpted characters and say the words of the characters. She was transparent about this process in her instructions to the class and added that if anyone else had something to add to the dialogue between mum and son, then they could get out of their place and add to it.

Manisha had well-established rules for talk so she knew that as this evolved into a more dramatic technique, she could still draw on the idea of silence, respect and focus while pupils were talking. She also decided to play some music at a low level to add to the sense of occasion and drama of the scene.

Once she had given the signal and the music had started, she signalled to the two pupils that they could leave their seats and stand behind the two sculpted characters and say their words, in role. She left a pause after this and looked encouragingly around the room to ascertain whether any other pupils felt confident enough to come up and add their words. Three pupils did so and layered on more of the tense dialogue between mum and Michael. She left a moment of reflection and paused before stopping the music and returning to her role as the facilitator of talk. She was careful at this point to ask the pupils who had spoken how they felt when they had stood behind the characters and whether it changed their view on either character. The pupils were still standing at this point and it added a more informal feeling to what was quite an in depth set of questions. She then asked the other pupils who were seated and observing if this had added anything to their understanding of the extract, of the characters and of their own feelings about the scene. Not all pupils were ready to respond but six different pupils contributed to this part of the discussion, the main observations being that they felt involved in the drama of the situation and felt sorry for the mum and Michael but for different reasons. She asked why these reasons were different even though the emotion was the same and two pupils referred back to the text to qualify the different situation of each character due to the parent/child relationship. A pupil, who had been observing up until this point, also asserted that he had not seen these emotions in the text but now he could as they were 'right in front of him'.

Manisha left the activity at this point as she was keen to finish it while the listening and engagement in the discussion was still high. Using mini-whiteboards, she then asked the pupils to write down an answer to the following question: 'How do you think Michael feels at this point and why?'

The pupils were keen to get their ideas on the boards and Manisha noted that many were rubbing out words and reforming their sentences. Moving around the room she was able to see that all pupils had something to say and were connected with the characters from an emotional point of view. While the degree of analysis was varied across the class, all pupils were able to engage with the why question and most referred back to the text to look for authorial clues. Today's activity had led the pupils towards answering a deep question and being able to do so with confidence and an investment in the text.

Before she moved on, Manisha explained how the pupils had engaged in a *thinking and feeling* activity and that both of these approaches would help them to build their interpretation skills. She also pointed out that there had been some different opinions about the text and that these were different interpretations. She normalised these difference knowing that she would be able to build on this in future chapters. This level of scaffolding continued to be an approach that Manisha adopted during the rest of the reading of the book as she planned for the pupils to gain greater confidence with interpreting texts.

Case study reflections

- How do you plan for emotional responses to text?
- How do you use drama approaches to develop empathy and understanding?
- What do you consider to be the benefits of building in collaborative meaning-making when interpreting texts?

The author/reader relationship

There has been a great deal of research on the author/reader relationship and how this feeds into the skill of interpretation. Reader response theory (Rosenblatt, 1983) relies on there being a relationship between the author and reader whereby there is a transaction, that is the reader engages as an active participant in making meaning (Barthes and Heath, 1977). That way, the reader might arrive at a different understanding of the meaning of the text as they may have viewed it differently (Sosa *et al.*, 2016). Once again, one can return to the consideration of the reader's world experience and knowledge, as they bring this into the encounter with text and therefore use it in this problem-solving task (Sosa *et al.*, 2016; Lee *et al.*, 2016).

Whitin (2005) explored the extent to which there was a relationship between sensory experiences and thinking. She was interested in the metaphorical representation that children could engage in if they responded to reading through pictures or diagrams. Transmediation, or the act of transferring text into a new medium, requires the learners to translate the connection between two ideas. Thus the young reader is actively involved in making meaning and has a relationship with the text. Barnes (1992) argued that this active participation is crucial in literary interpretation. Whitin (2005) found that the sketches themselves were not the end product in critical interpretation but that the conversations that pupils had about them afforded new insights, different questions and greater depth in their responses to the text.

Similarly, Knickerbocker and Rycik (2002) found that as pupils approached adolescence, there needed to be regular opportunities for them to build bridges between texts and to respond to the life issues that they found within texts. The oral interpretation was a vehicle to promote deeper insights as pupils were encouraged to talk through their ideas. It was the engagement with well-chosen texts that enabled pupils to invest their time and emotion in literature. Without this investment, pupils become disconnected from texts and are less likely to pursue a deeper exploration or response.

CASE STUDY

We will return now to Manisha's classroom to see how she has built on initial interpretation skills. Having continued to use dramatic approaches to interpretation throughout the reading of the novel, Manisha felt that the children were ready to experiment more transparently with the concept of interpretation. To that end, she chose a scene in the novel where Kensuke and Michael were saying goodbye to one another on the beach, before Michael went out to the boat to be reunited with his parents.

She organised the class so that they could sculpt the two characters into position at this moment in time, again taking due care to ensure that the pupils had access to the text for reference and exploration. Threading this approach to text through the unit of work had enabled the pupils to build up their reading stamina with close reading and articulating their opinions with reference to the text.

She then asked the pupils to consider the three-dimensional image and the feelings between the characters. She provided pairs with a strip of card and a felt tip pen to write down a word which described the space between the characters. She invited them up to place the card where they imagined the emotion to be and played music at the same time to evoke some of the dramatic feelings. Several pupils had written 'sad' and some had written 'excited' with reference to Michael's conflicting feelings as he prepared to be reunited with his parents. They placed their word on the other side of the sculpture of Michael, pointing towards the 'invisible' parents. Some pupils had written 'worried' or 'concerned' showing an understanding of the mutual respect and friendship which had developed between the two main characters.

Manisha was pleased with the initial emotional engagement that the pupils were showing and knew that she had built up their confidence with teacher questioning over the last few weeks when it came to deciding how they felt about a text. She asked pupils to think about where they would stand if they could move into the text itself, i.e. the three-dimensional image in front of them. She asked a specific individual to go and stand where they felt they viewed the text, as a reader. The boy moved towards 'Michael' and stood at his shoulder, explaining that he saw this situation from Michael's point of view: sad at leaving Kensuke but excited to see his parents. Manisha questioned another pupil to contribute and they stood by 'Kensuke' saying that the main emotion she could see was Kensuke's hurt and sense of loss. A few more pupils joined the group, standing in similar positions but offering different reasons or wording as to why they felt they were in this position as a reader.

Finally, Manisha had primed three of the more able children in the class to consider where they would stand to represent the point of view of the writer. She requested that they join the group and explain their choice of position. One child in particular decided to get a chair and stand on it, looking down at the interplay between 'Michael' and 'Kensuke', explaining that Morpurgo had built up two believable characters and that he had written about both of their experiences equally. At this point, Manisha handed all of the pupils standing in the centre of the circle a card with the word 'writer' or 'reader' on it in large letters, two different colours for each word. She invited the other pupils to get out of their seats and encircle the group, looking at the positions. As she requested that they all stood still, she told them that this sculpture was a three-dimensional version of the text and that they could see concrete versions of different interpretations of the text. Through her teacher commentary she was able to remind them that there were always different ways of 'reading' text and that our opinions would differ, hence there was a range of possible interpretations.

The following lesson, the pupils had some independent writing time to capture some of these discussions. Manisha set them up with a copy of the extract in front of them and an open question to consider: 'How did you react to the final parting of Michael and Kensuke and how did Morpurgo make you feel this way?' She encouraged them to write freely and to think about the 'sculpture' that they had seen and the words used to describe the space. She offered some pupils a more structured frame within which to write their thoughts. She was heartened to see that most pupils could articulate their own interpretations and that some had gone on to delve more deeply into their reasoning behind this.

Case study reflections

- How have you planned for the exploration of various interpretations?
- In what ways do you promote a potential divergence of the interpretations of reader and writer?
- How do you use questioning as a key part of teaching interpretation?

The case study above illustrates how you can plan to teach close reading and introduce more challenging texts if this follows collaborative and exploratory work with the text first.

Moving children towards interpreting texts with confidence

Speculation

Chambers (1993) advocated talk about books and asking open questions such as 'why', 'what', 'who', 'when' and 'where'. This allowed some speculation about the text and therefore opened up the reader's response without worrying about 'guessing' a required answer. Questions about why children liked or disliked a book could also promote such speculation in the early stages. With the right foundations for an open discussion, an engagement with personal interpretation is more likely. Evans (2016) went on to promote 'speculative ponderings' where she mused, 'I wonder what this means ...?' or 'I'm really unsure how this could have happened ... have you any ideas?' Again, this approach reminds children that there is no right or wrong and therefore implies that they can reason with meaning themselves and arrive at a personal interpretation. Think about where you offer opportunity for speculation or 'ponderings'. Do you have the right foundations for talk about text in the classroom?

Assessment

Throughout the explorations above you will have noted times when the role of teacher has facilitated the opportunity to assess pupils' progress. We will now consider some of these more explicitly here.

- *Questions for drama work.* During any drama work or active approaches to text, the teacher should pre-plan questions which will elicit deeper responses. Planning these in advance and targeting pupils accordingly will allow the teacher to build a picture of comprehension and interpretation which guides the next part of the lesson. Equally, it will tell of gaps in understanding that the teacher can rectify or direct the pupils to explore and solve themselves.

- *Placing the reader and the writer.* The drama activities described above are an excellent way to assess pupils' interpretative skills. They are live, three-dimensional models of how the pupils are interpreting pieces of text and should not be underestimated in the sequence of learning.

- *Listening to pupils' discussions about pictorial representations.* This is low-stakes assessment for pupils if time and effort has been spent creating a safe environment. At this point the teacher can not only see how the pupils have sketched a metaphorical response to the text but also see how they are able to articulate this to their peers.

- *Written work.* Following on from any of the case study experiences above will lead naturally into some form of writing to capture the pupils' interpretations. This might be more formal and structured around an open question about the text which requires the pupils to hypothesise and give an interpretation. Alternatively, it might be rooted in creative writing where they have to imagine that they are a character from the text. Not only will this begin with inference but it will move the children into thinking about a certain perspective regarding the plot development. How does this character react/behave differently to another character in similar circumstances? Do they have a different insight into how this character might be feeling?

CHAPTER SUMMARY

Within this chapter, we have explored how collaborative learning and drama work can create reliable foundations for pupils to offer a personal response to text. It is the opportunity to infer, share, sketch and sculpt their responses that affords developing readers the space to consider, muse, speculate and proffer their own insight to what they have read. All of this supports young, developing readers to understand the concept of interpretation.

Further reading

Bunyan, P and Moore, R (2005) *NATE drama packs introductory pack: Drama within English 11–16.* Sheffield: NATE.

Published by the National Association for the Teaching of English (NATE), these materials are well worth visiting for creative ideas on how to use some of the strategies described here and many others. Each scheme of work is accompanied by a teacher commentary, which is useful when approaching this for the first time and all strategies are easily adaptable to Key Stage 1 and Key Stage 2.

Cremin, T (2009) *Teaching English Creatively*. London: Taylor & Francis.

A useful text which explores what it means to teach creatively in primary schools.

References

Barnes, D (1992) *From Communication to Curriculum*. Portsmouth: Boynton/Cook.

Barthes, R and Heath, S (1977) *Image, Music, Text*. New York: Hill & Wang.

Chambers, A (1993) *Tell Me: Children, reading and talk*. Stroud: Thimble Press.

Department for Education (DfE) (2013) *National Curriculum in England: Framework for Key Stages 1 to 4*. London: DfE.

Eva-Wood, A (2004) How think-and-feel-aloud instruction influences poetry readers, *Discourse Processes, 38*: (2): 173–92.

Evans, J (2016) Who am I? Why am I here? and Where do I come from? Responding to philosophical picturebooks, *Education 3–13*, *44* (1): 53–67.

Fialho, O, Zyngier, S and Miall, D (2011) Interpretation and experience: two pedagogical interventions observed. *English in Education*, *45* (3): 236–53.

Knickerbocker, J and Rycik, J (2002) Growing into literature: Adolescents' literary interpretation and appreciation, *Journal of Adolescent and Adult Literacy*, *46*: 3.

Lee, CD, Goldman, SR, Levine, S and Magliano, J (2016). Epistemic cognition in literary reasoning, in JA Greene, WA Sandoval and I Braten (eds) *The Handbook of Epistemic Cognition*. New York: Routledge.

Levine, S (2014) Making interpretation visible with an affect-based strategy, *Reading Research Quarterly*, *49* (3): 283–303.

Morpurgo, M (2017) *Kensuke's Kingdom*. Egmont: London.

Rosenblatt, L (1983) *Literature as Exploration*, 4th edition. New York: Modern Language Association.

Sosa, T, Hall, A, Goldman, S and Lee, C (2016) Developing symbolic interpretation through literary argumentation, *Journal of the Learning Sciences*, *25* (1): 93–132.

Whitin, P (2005) The interplay of text, talk and visual representation in expanding literary interpretation, *Research in the Teaching of English*, *39* (4): 365–97.

9
THEMATIC APPROACHES

(Continued)

- maintain positive attitudes to reading and understanding of what they read by:
  - continuing to read and discuss an increasingly wide range of fiction, poetry, plays, non-fiction and reference books or textbooks
  - reading books that are structured in different ways and reading for a range of purposes
  - increasing their familiarity with a wide range of books, including myths, legends and traditional stories, modern fiction, fiction from our literary heritage, and books from other cultures and traditions
  - identifying and discussing themes and conventions in and across a wide range of writing
  - making comparisons within and across books
- understand what they read by:
  - drawing inferences such as inferring characters' feelings, thoughts and motives from their actions, and justifying inferences with evidence
  - summarising the main ideas drawn from more than one paragraph, identifying key details that support the main ideas
- participate in discussions about books that are read to them and those they can read for themselves, building on their own and others' ideas and challenging views courteously.

(DfE, 2013)

What do we mean by a thematic approach?

Thematic approaches to learning are based on integrating concepts, subjects, themes or texts in order to present learning in a contextual and holistic way, based on the premise that learners are more successful when engaged in learning in which connections can be easily made. It allows for greater creativity and challenge through the use of a varied and diverse range of teaching styles which can engage and enthuse learners, leading to a deeper understanding through active learning. However, the term 'thematic approach' is problematic in itself as it has come to have multiple meanings in education, some of which will be explored in this chapter.

Schools employ different approaches to thematic teaching, ranging from the use of text sets to develop deeper understanding to the implementation of schemes based around a significant text which allows children to enhance subject knowledge in a particular area. Indeed, a review of the current literature proposes many different definitions and derivatives of thematic teaching which differ in terms of purpose and aim. Some have their roots firmly attached to previous national curriculum requirements, for example the practice of using challenging texts to explore themes which ensures that quality texts lie *at the heart of the literacy curriculum* (Nicholson, 2006, p11). Others extol the virtues of text sets to widen background knowledge and improve comprehension skills (Lupo *et al.*, 2017; Gelzheiser *et al.*, 2014). There is also a more historical body of research that explores cross-curricular teaching through the use of a thematic approach, which Shanahan refers to as *integrated instruction* (Shanahan, 1997, p12), as it allows pupils opportunities to make connections across various disciplines and promotes a deeper understanding of subject knowledge (Lipson *et al.*, 1993; Tyler, 1992).

Theme-led approach

The theme of a book, not to be confused with the moral of the story, infiltrates all corners of the narrative and sits at the heart of a story. If we understand the plot to be about the events that take place within a period of time, the theme must surely be the backbone that runs through, linking character, action and setting in such a way as to allow the reader to immerse themselves fully in the text. I am sure we can all remember reading a book which resonated deeply with our own values and beliefs, challenging our assumptions and extending our thoughts around human nature. *Journey to Jo'Burg* by Beverley Naidoo and *The Terrible Thing That Happened to Barnaby Brocket* by John Boyne were two such texts that challenged my own perceptions as I explored uncomfortable themes, integrating new information with prior knowledge. What we bring to a text in terms of knowledge and experience will have a lasting impact upon how we understand and remember what we read (Blachowicz and Ogle, 2014). Therefore it follows that pupils will interact more willingly with texts when they believe that they relate specifically to their own values and goals (Wigfield *et al.*, 2016). The use of the following two questions are key when initiating discussions around themes:

- What does the author want us to think about?

- What are your views on this?

This will allow pupils to summarise the key themes and assimilate them into their own values system, justifying their opinions based on prior knowledge and experiences – an important skill when comprehending texts. An appreciation of the themes contained in a text allows a richer discussion around characters' motives, actions and thoughts which inevitably enhance comprehension skills and challenges the reader to read beyond what is obvious.

Quality text approach

Engaging readers is key to improving reading attainment (Baker and Wigfield, 1999; Twist *et al.*, 2012; Petscher, 2010). Therefore it is imperative that we explore how reading practices can support this motivation in the classroom and beyond. One such approach would be to employ a pedagogy which capitalises on pupils' interests and experiences: something with which pupils can connect. Choosing the right book is crucial in fostering the motivation to read and the exploration of themes within such books is a key component of the national curriculum as pupils should be taught to identify and discuss themes and conventions introduced in a variety of texts (DfE, 2013). Finding a book that appeals to 'good readers' can make all the difference, especially if it is a theme with which they can identify; for example friendship, kindness, uniqueness. Making personal connections, based on prior knowledge, experience and understanding can have an impact on pupils' ability to critically read a text which will, in turn, enhance comprehension skills (Adams and Bushman, 2006). Furthermore, when this text is particularly challenging, it may have a positive effect on motivation to read (Shanahan *et al.*, 2012).

Planning a thematic approach

Using a strong text to explore themes is one way in which we can challenge readers in terms of comprehension and knowledge – the exploration of a theme brings relevance to the discussion. When themes are connected to character development, pupils must go beyond what is obvious in the text and extract meaning in order to comment on characters' motives, actions and thoughts. Discussion and debate which centre around these themes can allow pupils to deepen understanding of a text so that they can infer and draw conclusions based on the evidence. Sometimes this is buried beneath layers of meaning within the text and requires skilful questioning to bring it to the forefront. In addition, it is important that, as texts become increasingly more challenging, pupils *expand their vocabularies and knowledge base, and learn to use elaborate cognitive strategies to make inferences and analyse text critically* (Wigfield *et al.*, 2016, p190). Therefore exploring theme through a key text requires careful planning.

CASE STUDY: *WONDER* BY RJ PALACIO

This case study explores how the use of a quality text to explore theme:

1.	developed comprehension skills;
2.	initiated high-level discussion and debate.

Kathryn came across *Wonder* by RJ Palacio when she was teaching a Year 6 class and decided to introduce it to pupils as a class text during whole-class reading sessions. There had been several incidents of friends falling out within her class and she wanted a unifying theme to help address some of the issues. Therefore she started with a book which presented strong themes and planned ideas around this in order to engage her pupils and challenge their thinking.

For Kathryn, it was important that the themes were relevant to pupils' values and beliefs as she knew this would enhance learning, therefore she started by initiating a discussion around what it meant to be a good friend. Because August Pullman, the main character in *Wonder*, is different in appearance due to his facial disfigurement, his classmates have to look beyond this to appreciate what he is truly like inside. Kathryn wanted to capitalise on this to encourage her own class to look beneath the surface and respect each other for who they were, at the same time exploring themes of:

- friendship
- identity
- bullying
- self-image
- kindness.

Kathryn started with the two questions which she posed to the whole class:

- What makes a good friend?
- How do you know that you are a good friend?

This led to pupils formulating a list of qualities associated with friendship and examining their own values and actions. She followed this up by asking children to identify a particular time when they had been a good friend and what this had felt like.

She introduced the text to her class using the quote from the book cover:

You can't blend in when you were born to stand out.

She asked them to discuss what they thought it meant. Responses were varied and allowed Kathryn to not only assess prior knowledge, but to plan key lines of enquiry that she could build upon in her lessons. Some children felt that it was important not to stand out whereas others discussed this as a good thing. Questions raised included: Should you only stand out for good things? Do we mean physical or hidden attributes? How does personality affect how we stand out? What happens to those people who stand out? Are they successful for standing out? What impact do they have on other people? What makes someone 'stand out'? All of the questions were recorded and added to the working wall to allow children to ponder over them during the week.

Kathryn went on to read *Wonder* with her class and developed their knowledge of theme through key questions which allowed pupils to engage on a much deeper level with the characters (Table 9.1).

Table 9.1   *Key questions used in the exploration of themes in RJ Palacio's Wonder*

Theme	Key questions
Bullying	How do you feel about 'the neutrals'? Is this acceptable? How does it differ from bullying? How does Via's advice to Auggie differ from Jack's actions? Which is more acceptable and why?
Kindness	Mr Tushman's 'middle school address' centres on kindness. Do you agree when he asks, 'shall we make a new rule of life … always try to be a little kinder than is necessary'? Why? What do you think this means?
	When Henry, Miles and Amos stick up for Auggie, does it change Auggie's opinion of them? In what ways?
Self-image	What does beauty look like? What do we mean by 'normal'?
	Does the way in which Auggie's parents treat him impact upon his self-image? Is this always right?
Friendship	Is Summer's loyalty more important than Jack's friendship? Why/why not? How important is forgiveness in the development of Jack and Auggie's relationship?
Identity	How does the character of Via develop through the course of the story – does she achieve the recognition she craves and how does this change the way she feels about her brother?
	How do you think Auggie feels about himself when starting school?
	Is this different from when he was home-schooled? Why/why not?
	How does Julian see himself, do you think? Does this change as the story progresses? How?

(Continued)

(Continued)

Key passages were explored in more detail, looking at how symbols and motifs within the book strengthened the themes. For example, throughout the book, there are references to 'beauty' which Kathryn was able to explore with pupils in terms of identity and self-image. The opening of part eight in the book quotes lyrics from the Eurythmics:

You're gonna reach the sky

Fly ... Beautiful Child

(Eurythmics, *Beautiful Child*)

This led to work around the concept of 'beauty' and what it meant to individuals. Pupils also explored it from characters' points of view, using evidence from the text to justify their reasoning. This culminated in pupils producing a piece of writing about their chosen character which demonstrated that pupils could understand what they read by *drawing inferences such as inferring characters' feelings, thoughts and motives from their actions, and justifying inferences with evidence* (DfE, 2013, p34). Using open and structured discussion, Kathryn had explored themes within the book and used this to engage and motivate readers. They were able to connect with the characters through the use of themes, which in turn led to pupils becoming critical readers, a key skill when developing comprehension (Adams and Bushman, 2006, p27).

Case study reflections

- How do you select quality texts to use in the classroom?
- Consider how you plan to use theme to develop criticality in reading.
- How do you use questioning to engage pupils in debate and discussion around key themes?

From the case study above, it is clear that relevance has a significant impact upon pupils' engagement. The themes running through *Wonder* are universal and relevant to children's own experiences, although the way in which they are explored in the book may not be. Pupils may not have had direct experience of befriending a child such as Auggie, but they will be familiar with kindness, friendship and identity and have opinions as to what this looks like. By introducing common themes through unfamiliar situations, pupils are forced to assimilate this into their existing knowledge framework leading to rich discussion around motives and character development. When reading texts, we often ask children to identify a character's motives and provide examples as to why they have acted in a particular way. By encouraging the pupils in her class to explore their own actions, Kathryn was establishing a basis for reading the text, extending vocabulary, encouraging justification and allowing pupils to evaluate the consequences of their actions. As teachers, we are very aware of the importance of questioning and discussion which allow children to co-construct knowledge (Alexander, 2004) and is a useful exercise to undertake prior to examining the text as it motivates pupils to want to find out more. Good readers are those that actively construct meaning through linking what they read to what they already know (Blachowicz and Ogle, 2014) and by spending time exploring pupils' opinions and views prior to engaging with a text we can stimulate this knowledge and enhance learning.

Using text sets to develop comprehension

Exploring themes through the use of multiple texts can lead to greater success in developing comprehension skills (Alvermann and Wilson, 2011; Ciecierski and Bintz, 2016), particularly when teaching what we might class as 'more able' readers. Connected texts can lead to greater criticality as pupils link ideas and synthesise information to explore texts on a much deeper level. It allows pupils to explore multiple narratives, examine text structure and question authorial intent. Interpretation, evaluation and application are all skills that can be enhanced through the use of text sets which link themes in such a way as to engage and enthuse the reader.

Text sets are collections of texts from varied genres, which have a central topic which runs throughout. They are predominantly used to build subject knowledge in a structured and consistent manner, focusing on key concepts rather than content which leads to greater comprehension. By reading several texts that are connected by a unifying concept, pupils are able to benefit from a broader perspective and a deeper level of analysis. Indeed, research has demonstrated the success of using multiple texts to extend knowledge and widen vocabulary – two key areas of reading comprehension (Cervetti *et al.*, 2016). Prior knowledge can have a more successful effect on reading comprehension than pupil's reading ability because subject knowledge can influence understanding (Arya *et al.*, 2011). As pupils develop subject knowledge through exposure to connected texts, they are able to use this successfully when exposed to a more challenging text which requires a greater degree of analysis.

The importance of early language experiences in developing comprehension skills has long been established (Bishop and Snowling, 2004; Catts *et al.*, 2012), therefore providing time for children to talk to and listen to each other will contribute towards building vocabulary which will in turn aid comprehension. The use of multiple texts can enhance this and are useful tools in expanding a reader's knowledge base and exposure to rich vocabulary through increasing the time that pupils are exposed to reading, thus producing a 'rich get richer' effect in terms of attainment in reading (Stanovich, 2008, p23).

RESEARCH FOCUS: THE MATTHEW EFFECT

The Matthew effect of accumulated advantage as described in sociology is a phenomenon by which 'the rich get richer and poor get poorer'. It was a concept originally used by sociologist Robert Merton in his work. The effect has its origins in the Bible as it is from the Parable of Talents in the Gospel of Matthew. Stanovich adopted this term for education when writing about how those children who are vocabulary and knowledge rich at an early developmental stage continue to develop in terms of attainment in reading (Stanovich, 1986). Those children who read less have poorer comprehension skills which serve to 'widen the gap' between themselves and their peers over time.

Research has shown that children within the lowest quartile for vocabulary development have significantly reduced vocabularies when compared with those in the top quartile (Biemiller and

(Continued)

(Continued)

Slomin, 2001). In 1988, Anderson *et al.* estimated that those children who read for longer periods of time will come across four million words a year as compared with those who do not read regularly, who may only meet around 50,000 words within the same time period. A more recent study concluded that by the time a child reaches the age of three, there is already a 30 million word gap between children from the wealthiest and poorest families (Colker, 2014). This will have significant impact upon children's comprehension skills as children who read more frequently will be exposed to a greater number of words which will afford them greater opportunities to extend knowledge (Cain and Oakhill, 2011).

Selecting Texts
- What do pupils need to know? What skills do you want to develop?
- Find texts that will support the learning.
- Select texts from a wide variety of genres; eg, information, poetry, visual, images, art

Organising texts
- Which text will you use to 'hook in' your readers?
- Which text becomes your target text? This should be a more challenging text in terms of vocabulary and subject knowledge as it will be the culminating text.
- How will you intoroduce your supplementary texts?

Developing knowledge
- What is the key content to be explored?
- Levels of vocabulary -how will they be introduced?
- What strategies will you employ to develop knowledge?

Synthesising information
- Plan meaningful learning opportunities that allow pupils time to discuss the information they have assimilated
- Provide scaffolds for children to comprehend a more challenging text using prior knowledge

Planning to use text sets in the classroom

The use of multiple texts to explore theme should provide pupils with increasing opportunities to engage with different types of writing. Reading challenging texts can lead to greater success which can be motivating in itself (Shanahan *et al.*, 2012), especially for readers who are already exhibiting high levels of competence in comprehension. However, the use of texts with varying levels of difficulty could engage a greater number of readers as an informed choice of texts is crucial to success in teaching across the ability range. Lupo *et al.* suggest that the order in which texts are introduced to pupils is important in building knowledge and fostering engagement as the use of more accessible texts motivates readers to attempt more challenging texts (Lupo *et al.*, 2017).

The national curriculum for English states that pupils should be able to identify and discuss *themes and conventions in and across a wide range of writing* and make *comparisons within and across books* (DfE, 2013, p34). The use of text sets facilitates such skills and will lead pupils to greater levels of subject knowledge and criticality through familiarity with vocabulary, ideas and concepts while contextualising learning.

A suggested framework for planning the use of text sets

CASE STUDY

Sandeep was eager to introduce her class to a more complex text as she wanted to explore themes and characters using something more challenging. She had read about the use of multiple texts across a range of genres to increase engagement and interaction with more challenging narratives and decided to plan a series of lessons around a target text, supplemented with a number of subsidiary texts which could be used to build knowledge and explore vocabulary.

Target text: *Animal Farm* by George Orwell

Supplementary texts:

- *Charlotte's Web* by EB White (a more accessible text)
- **www.bbc.co.uk/newsround/41904621** - background on the Russian Revolution
- **http://flavorwire.com/205115/100-year-old-color-photographs-from-the-russian-empire/4** - visual resource for pupils to study photographs from the Russian Revolution
- **www.storyboardthat.com/teacher-guide/animal-farm-by-george-orwell** - storyboard which enabled pupils to access a visual representation of a complex text.

(Continued)

(Continued)

Themes:

- Equality and inequality
- Power
- Conflict
- Friendship

Sandeep employed the model above to begin planning how she would introduce the texts. Consequently, she was able to teach the different texts in an order which would promote the greatest success in learning. Pupils had a greater understanding of the historical and political context through the use of information texts and she was able to engage pupils in rich discussion based around the themes.

Case study reflections

- How do you plan to build on pupils' existing knowledge?
- Consider the use of scaffolds to support all learners in the acquisition of skills and knowledge.
- What meaningful learning opportunities will you provide to extend learning?

Challenges

Controversial themes

As pupils engage with more complex and challenging texts, there is greater exposure to what some may consider more controversial themes. These may include race, bereavement, mental health, gender identity and domestic abuse. Malorie Blackman's *Noughts and Crosses* explores race from a different perspective; *Us Minus Mum* by Heather Butler is a beautifully written book about how George and Theo come to terms with their loss while Sarah Crossan's *The Weight of Water* tackles the subject of alienation and immigration. All are written for young readers and explore some of the more challenging aspects of the world around us. It is important that you, as the teacher, know your pupils before introducing such texts. Creating an environment that is 'safe' and an ethos that is positive will lead to confident and informed discussion. We need to support our pupils to develop skills such as empathy, reasoning and critical thinking in order to enhance comprehension skills and this can be somewhat more disconcerting when sensitive issues are being explored. However, careful planning of questions, secure knowledge of pupils' backgrounds and careful selection of texts will support children's learning in these areas.

Tenuous links

Sometimes in our quest to ensure learning is meaningful, it is useful to employ a cross-curricular approach for, as Shanahan is quick to point out, there is a compelling body of evidence that suggests it increases motivation, meaning and a deeper understanding (Shanahan, 1997). However, these studies are somewhat dated and may have had more relevance when teaching to a national curriculum that has since been superseded. Good readers are able to construct knowledge through linking ideas, integrating what they know and applying this to new subjects or topics. Sometimes, when we plan with a theme in mind, it can be the topic that leads the learning rather than the linking of skills, understanding and knowledge across disciplines. Sometimes teachers struggle to shoehorn topics into subjects, negating any of the positive effects of a thematic approach. It is, therefore, crucial that purposeful learning remains at the heart of thematic teaching if it is to be successful. Systematic planning which considers children's interests, abilities and understanding will build knowledge and allow pupils to make the links and connections with other areas of the curriculum which ensures learning remains relevant.

Engagement and motivation

Correct choice of themes and texts will have a significant effect on pupils' learning in terms of motivating them to read more widely. Themes that are relevant to their own lives, interests and experiences will lead to greater engagement (Wigfield *et al.*, 2016; Assor *et al.*, 2002) which will ultimately enhance learning and develop comprehension skills. When asking your class to choose a theme or a text, be mindful that it may not appeal to every learner. I once visited a classroom where the children were studying Ancient Greeks using *Jason and the Argonauts* as a key text. While many of the children were enjoying the text, and could talk knowledgeably about plot, characters and setting, there was a group of more able girls who admitted that they were not engaging with the content and found it 'boring'. How you engage and motivate pupils using relevant texts or themes is crucial in developing learning – ensuring that you provide a breadth of reading materials will help to address this.

> *Instruction that makes few attempts to spark children's interest and features unappealing texts can decrease intrinsic motivation. If teachers restrict students' choice of reading topics or materials too much, they risk stifling intrinsic motivation and autonomy.*

(Wigfield *et al.*, 2016, p191)

Assessment

Assessing key skills around themes enables teachers to evaluate pupils' knowledge and understanding in this area. The ability to discuss themes and analyse these across a wide range of written materials is a vital component of the statutory requirements of the national curriculum (DfE, 2013). In order to facilitate this and provide practitioners with the necessary information to progress learning, assessment needs to take place. This can be done in a number of ways:

- *Text annotation.* Using significant passages from the text or multiple texts, pupils can comment on what the author is trying to say about the theme. Exploring authorial intent in this way will allow pupils to demonstrate a deeper understanding of the text. Connecting a theme to character development will also allow pupils to comment on characters' motives using evidence from the text to support this.

- *Summarising key themes.* Tweet the theme of the book. This requires pupils to use only 280 characters which will inevitably encourage them to think carefully about their choice of words and phrases. If pupils can do this succinctly, it will provide you, as the teacher, with information to assess whether pupils have a deeper understanding of the text.

- *Reader response activities.* Use book groups to allow pupils to discuss their interpretation of the themes within a range of books. By listening in, you will gain a greater understanding of their insights and perspectives. This allows learners to participate in discussions about books ... they can read for themselves, building on their own and others' ideas and challenging views courteously (DfE, 2013, p34).

- *Writing from the author's point of view.* Asking pupils to write from the author's perspective about their intention encourages them to 'step inside the author's shoes' and justify their thinking.

- *Key questions.* Questions which allow pupils to share and reconstruct their understanding will elicit responses which can aid assessment. Use the following questions to assess understanding:

  o How do you know that?

  o What makes you think that?

  o What does this character tell us about that one?

  o How do they change through the course of the book?

  o What do you think the author wants us to feel at this point?

  o What lasting opinions do you have now you have finished the book?

  o What did the author want us to think about?

  o How might you persuade a friend to read this book?

  o Why is this episode important in the story? For the story? For the character?

─── CHAPTER SUMMARY ───

This chapter provides information around developing comprehension skills through the use of thematic approaches. It draws upon a wide range of research and expert opinion to enable the reader to draw their own conclusions based on an analysis of current thinking. Children are engaged, motivated and learn more when teaching is relevant to their own experiences. By allowing pupils to make these connections, we are able to extend vocabulary, build subject knowledge and encourage inference - all of which are crucial for developing reading comprehension.

Further reading

Book Trust website: **https://www.booktrust.org.uk/**

Useful lists of connected texts to use with a wide range of year groups.

Evans, J (ed.) (2015) *Challenging and Controversial Picture Books*. Abingdon: Routledge.

Useful for extending subject knowledge around teaching controversial themes through children's books.

Newton, L (ed.) (2012) *Creativity for a New Curriculum*. London: David Fulton.

Lots of ideas for developing the use of texts in the classroom.

References

Adams, J and Bushman, J (2006) Thematic solutions using young adult literature to increase reading comprehension, *Middle School Journal, 37* (4): 25–9.

Alexander, R (2004) *Towards Dialogic Teaching: Rethinking classroom talk*. York: Dialogos UK.

Alvermann, DE and Wilson, AA (2011) Comprehension strategy instruction for multimodal texts in science, *Theory into Practice, 50* (2): 116–24.

Anderson, RC, Wilson, PT and Fielding, LG (1988) Growth in reading and how children spend their time outside of school, *Reading Research Quarterly, 13*: 285–303.

Arya, DJ, Hiebert, EH and Pearson, PD (2011) The effects of syntactic and lexical complexity on the comprehension of elementary science texts, *International Electronic Journal of Elementary Education, 4* (1): 107–25.

Assor, A, Kaplan, H and Roth, G (2002) Choice is good, but relevance is excellent: Autonomy-enhancing and suppressing teacher behaviors predicting students' engagement in schoolwork, *British Journal of Educational Psychology, 72*: 261–78.

Baker, L and Wigfield, A (1999) Dimensions of children's motivation for reading and their relations to reading activity and reading achievement, *Reading Research Quarterly, 34* (4): 452–76.

Biemiller, A and Slomin, N (2001) Estimating root word vocabulary growth in normative and advantaged populations: Evidence for a common sequence of vocabulary acquisition, *Journal of Educational Psychology, 93* (3): 498–520.

Bishop, D and Snowling, M (2004) Developmental dyslexia and specific language impairment: Same or different? *Psychological Bulletin, 130*: 858–86.

Blachowicz, CLZ and Ogle, D (2014) *Reading Comprehension: Strategies for independent learners*. New York: Guilford Publications.

Blackman, M (2001) *Noughts and Crosses*. London: Random House.

Boyne, J (2013) *The Terrible Thing that Happened to Barnaby Brocket*. London: Random House.

Butler, H (2014) *Us minus Mum*. London: Little Brown Books.

Cain, K and Oakhill, J (2011) Matthew effects in young readers: Reading comprehension and reading experience aid vocabulary development, *Journal of Learning Disabilities*, *44* (5): 431–43.

Catts, H, Kamhi, A and Adlof, S (2012) Defining and classifying reading disabilities, in A Kamhi and HW Catts (eds) *Language and Reading Disabilities*, 3rd edition. Boston, MA: Allyn & Bacon, pp 45–76.

Cervetti, G, Wright, T and Hwang, H (2016) Conceptual coherence, comprehension, and vocabulary acquisition: A knowledge effect? *Reading and Writing: An Interdisciplinary Journal*, *29* (4): 761–79.

Ciecierski, L and Bintz, WP (2016) Paired texts: A way into the content area, *Middle School Journal*, *47* (4): 32–44.

Colker, LJ (2014) The word gap: The early years make the difference, *Teaching Young Children*, *7* (3): 26–8.

Crossan, S (2012) *The Weight of Water*. London: Bloomsbury.

Department for Education (DfE) (2013) *The National Curriculum in England: Framework for Key Stages 1 to 4*. London: DfE.

Gelzheiser, L, Hallgren-Flynn, L, Connors, M and Scanlon, D (2014) Reading thematically related texts to develop knowledge and comprehension, *Reading Teacher*, *69* (1): 53–6.

Lipson, M, Valencia, S, Wixson, K and Peters, C (1993) Integration and thematic teaching: Integration to improve teaching and learning, *Language Arts*, *70* (1): 252– 63.

Lupo, S, Strong, J, Lewis, W, Walpole S and McKenna, M (2017) Building background knowledge through reading: Rethinking text sets, *Adolescent and Adult Literacy*, *61* (4): 433–44.

Naidoo, B (2016) *Journey to Jo'Burg*. London: HarperCollins.

Nicholson, D (2006) Putting literature at the heart of the literacy curriculum, *Literacy*, *40* (1): 11–21.

Orwell, G (2000 edition) *Animal Farm*. London: Penguin.

Palacio, RJ (2014) *Wonder*. London: Random House.

Petscher, Y (2010) A meta-analysis of the relationship between student attitudes towards reading and achievement in reading, *Journal of Research in Reading*, *33* (4): 335–55.

Shanahan, T (1997) Reading-writing relationships, thematic units, inquiry learning … In pursuit of effective integrated literacy instruction, *Reading Teacher*, *51* (1): 12–19.

Shanahan, T, Fisher, D and Frey, N (2012) The challenge of challenging text, *Educational Leadership*, *69* (6): 58–62.

Stanovich, K (1986) Matthew effects in reading: Some consequences of individual differences in the acquisition of literacy, *Reading Research Quarterly*, *21*: 360–406.

Stanovich, K (2008) Matthew effects in reading: Some consequences of individual differences in the acquisition of literacy, *Journal of Education*, *189*: 23–55.

Twist, L, Sizmur, J, Bartlett, S and Lynn, L (2012) PIRLS 2011: Reading Achievement in England. Slough: NFER.

Tyler, K (1992) Differentiation and integration of the primary curriculum, *Journal of Curriculum Studies*, *24* (6): 563–7.

Wigfield, A, Gladstone, J and Turci, L (2016) Beyond cognition: Reading motivation and reading comprehension, *Child Development Perspectives*, *10* (3): 190–5.

10
READING AND ASSESSMENT

CHAPTER OBJECTIVES

This chapter will allow you to achieve the following outcomes:

- Understand what statutory assessment looks like for reading at Key Stage 2;
- Explore different methods of formative assessment around reading;
- Consider relevant research around assessing reading comprehension.

LINKS TO THE TEACHERS' STANDARDS

Working through this chapter will help you meet the following standards:

1. Set high expectations which inspire, motivate and challenge pupils

2. Promote good progress and outcomes by pupils

5. Adapt teaching to respond to the strengths and needs of all pupils

6. Make accurate and productive use of assessment

LINKS TO THE NATIONAL CURRICULUM

Years five and six Programme of Study

Reading – comprehension

Pupils should be taught to:

- maintain positive attitudes to reading and an understanding of what they read by:

  o continuing to read and discuss an increasingly wide range of fiction, poetry, plays, non-fiction and reference books or textbooks

  o recommending books that they have read to their peers, giving reasons for their choices

  o identifying and discussing themes and conventions in and across a wide range of writing

  o making comparisons within and across books

- understand what they read by:

  o checking that the book makes sense to them, discussing their understanding and exploring the meaning of words in context

  o asking questions to improve their understanding

  o drawing inferences such as inferring characters' feelings, thoughts, and motives from their actions, and justifying inferences with evidence

  o predicting what might happen from details stated and implied

  o summarising the main ideas drawn from more than 1 paragraph, identifying key details that support the main ideas

  o identifying how language, structure and presentation contribute to meaning

- discuss and evaluate how authors use language, including figurative language, considering the impact on the reader

- distinguish between statements of fact and opinion

- retrieve, record and present information from non-fiction

- participate in discussions about books that are read to them and those they can read for themselves, building on their own and others' ideas and challenging views courteously

- explain and discuss their understanding of what they have read, including through formal presentations and debates, maintaining a focus on the topic, and using notes where necessary

- provide reasoned justifications for their views

DfE (2013)

Teachers should be assessing to determine both progress and to ascertain any 'gaps' and competences, to inform future progress. In its recent report, The Education Endowment Foundation states: *Adapting teaching and learning based on high quality information, collected through observation and assessment, can support all children by ensuring that the challenge and support that they receive is appropriate* (EEF, 2018, p6). Assessing reading comprehension can be challenging at all stages, but particularly for the advanced readers where depth of knowledge is important; especially as many of the cognitive processes that contribute to reading comprehension are not always obvious and therefore cannot be directly observed or measured (Snowling *et al.*, 2009, p3). Assessment has featured in each chapter of this book; this chapter will build on some of the features of assessment discussed in previous chapters and will aim to support teachers to identify those key features of children who are reading at a higher level.

Assessment: Why? What? When?

Why do we assess?

As with all subjects, teachers should be assessing readers to know what they can do to target next steps. The DfE is clear in the use of the purpose; 'why' we assess.

The purpose of assessment

Schools should develop their own approach to assessment which meets the needs of their pupils, parents, staff and curriculum. Statutory teacher assessment at the end of the key stage is just one part of the broader assessments that teachers make. There are three main forms of assessment in schools:

1. **Day-to-day formative assessment** - to inform teaching on an ongoing basis
2. **In-school summative assessment** - to understand pupil performance at the end of a period of teaching
3. **National statutory summative assessment** - to understand pupil performance in relation to national expectations and comparisons.

In the context of statutory teacher assessment, it is a school's own assessment policy which forms the basis of a teacher's judgements about what pupils know and can do. This will provide the evidence upon which teachers make a judgement against the statutory teacher assessment frameworks, which are designed only to report an outcome to government at the end of the key stage.

Statutory teacher assessment, as one measure of pupil performance, helps teachers and parents to understand broadly what a pupil can do in relation to national expectations, and allows the government to hold schools to account for the education they provide to their pupils. However, pupils will have a wider range of knowledge and skills than that covered by statutory assessment. This may be evident through other forms of assessment that take place at school and should be reported to parents (STA, 2018, p8).

What do we assess?

The multi-faceted skills required for successful comprehension have been the focus of this book which means the methods of assessing comprehension can be equally as complex. But how can this be assessed? What should be assessed to understand this? In short, teachers should be using a multitude of methods to determine whether:

*   children can read the words on the page

*   they can apply meaning in that particular (local) context

- they can begin to apply meaning to a wider (global) context

- readers can make use of wider knowledge to make sense of implied detail

(Snowling *et al.*, 2009)

When do we assess?

Statutory testing will obviously dictate 'when' for some year groups, and schools may have their own summative assessment procedures which will also be part of the school calendar. As with any lesson, sharing clear learning objectives with the children; a shared, clear picture of what that successful learning looks like; a positive classroom where 'trying' is valued; support for pupils to reflect on their own learning, and feedback that supports the next steps are instrumental to progress and the assessment process. This could be as often as daily, or ongoing. Ideally, reading, including comprehension, should be assessed regularly to provide relevant information to plan for future learning – ideally, with the child.

Assessment of Reading Comprehension at Key Stage 2

Statutory Summative Assessment of Reading at KS2

In terms of reading, from 2015 to July 2018, Key Stage 2 teachers were expected to make teacher assessments of reading using the Interim Assessment Framework (DfE, 2017a). This was alongside the statutory Key Stage 2 reading test; schools were expected to report both teacher assessed reading and the test results. From September 2018, the Teacher Assessment expectation was withdrawn, and pupils' assessment of reading is now judged only by the statutory test. This change was partly due to the drive to reduce teacher workload. Of course, this now means that reading comprehension attainment can only be reported through the test, essentially pupils' written responses to a text under timed conditions, which conflicts with much of the theory around what 'good comprehension' is (Keenan, 2016). The Key Stage 2 SATs reading test also does not consider some of the National Curriculum reading comprehension objectives that should be taught, namely those with 'discussion' as part of the wording. Schools must therefore ensure that teachers are confident in how to plan and assess these areas, not for reporting nationally, but to ensure progress.

Summative Assessment of Reading at KS2

At school level, other summative methods may be chosen. Reading tests such as NFER - Nelson, YARC (York Assessment for Reading Comprehension) and Accelerated Reader are all marketed as tools for assessing children's comprehension which can be useful for 'measuring' comprehension. However, using such tests exclusively to determine a child's comprehension strengths can be misleading (Snowling *et al*, 2009). For example, each test differs in the amount of text that is required to be read: from simple sentences to extended passages. Multiple-choice questions or true-false questions require a different cognitive process to writing developed answers. They have been criticised for relying on low level comprehension skills (Klingner, 2004) focusing on recall and questions around the main ideas in a text, rather than the layers of meaning. Some tests were *very highly dependent on decoding* (Snowling *et al*, 2009, p4) which of course is a barrier for some children and does not always correlate with their comprehension ability. Schools, however, use them as a comparison or a benchmark for all children in a school. Other summative assessment methods may be end of module/topic 'testing', conducted as a question/answer session or using IT such as Kahoot quizzes (see https://kahoot.com/).

The KS2 Content Domain

Chapter 4 and chapter 6 both detail the Key Stage 2 Content Domains (STA, 2016) and its relevance in terms of summative statutory assessment. The key verbs from the content domain (give/explain/retrieve/record/identify/infer/justify/predict/compare) are all indications of effective comprehension and chapter 6 suggests a series of question stems which are useful for both teaching and assessing comprehension. In terms of assessment, it is useful to be aware of these verbs and use them to shape your assessment tasks.

How to identify a 'good comprehender'

How do we know whether a child is working at the expected standard or even beyond (there is no 'working at greater depth' for reading at KS2 as there is for writing)? Figure 10.1 is a transcript from STA's exemplification of standards. It shows a pupil's written response focusing on the use of language in 'The Executioner's Daughter' by Jane Hardstaff (2016). (DfE, 2017b).

The report reflects that the child is at the expected standard for the following reasons:

- *The pupil can explain reasons for the author's choice of vocabulary, and the impact that it has on the reader. For example, he links his knowledge of volcanoes to the dramatic entrance of Mrs Peak, commenting on the image of her explosive force as words spit from her mouth.*

- *Alternative meanings are offered for the word 'filthy', demonstrating that the pupil has not only considered the context of the text, but has attempted to link meaning to prior knowledge.*

- *In explaining Nell's grin, the pupil makes a plausible inference, based on the actions and words of the characters; the supposition that Nell 'didn't care' shows understanding of her disdain for Mrs Peak.*

- *In the final response, the pupil recognises that the words are not intended to be taken literally, and that the 'sort of expression' of speech is used to emphasise her abhorrence of the smell. (STA, 2016)*

Q. Why do you think the author used the word 'erupted' to describe Mrs Peak's entrance into the courtyard?

P. Because it makes her sound explosive like a volcano erupts and you can imagine her spitting the words out of her mouth like the lava and rocks.

Q. Mrs Peak describes the rat-catcher as 'filthy'. What do you think the word 'filthy' means in this passage?

P. It could mean that he was always dirty like he never washes, and his clothes are all smelly ...

Also, it might mean that he had a bad temper because you can have a filthy temper which means it's really bad.

Q. Why did Nell grin at Moss?

P. Mrs Peak kept making a lot of fuss about nothing and it was a sort of signal to show Moss she didn't care and she thought Mrs Peak was quite funny when she was shouting at everyone.

Q. The cook says, "Someone cut off my nose!" What does she mean by this?

P. I think it's a sort of expression because she doesn't want somebody to really cut off her nose but she can smell something horrible in the kitchen and she's exaggerating how bad it is. (STA, 2016)

Figure 10.1   'Expected Standard' at KS2

This evidence was used to demonstrate what the 'expected' standard could look like. Since September 2018 there are no 'Pupil can' statements to indicate this standard as there is no expectation to report teacher assessment. However, the exemplification materials continue to be useful.

Another useful resource has been produced by CLPE (2016), which uses research to produce a 'reading scale' which supports teachers to define where readers are situated on a scale of independence in reading (see Figure 10.2). The scale defines what behaviours a reader might demonstrate at that particular reading stage. Suggestions are outlined as to next steps in order to ensure progression. This is particularly useful for teachers who may need guidance as to the next stage of reading.

Again, the wording for each stage links to the research already discussed in previous chapters and the content domain. At the very highest independent level of reading, teachers should be providing assessment opportunities for students who should demonstrate:

- Critical reflection

- Engagement with a wide variety of texts

- The ability to make comparisons across texts

- Depth of awareness of authors' language choice

- The ability to discuss the reliability of a text

- Reflection on the relationship between any pictures and text or the layout and its effect

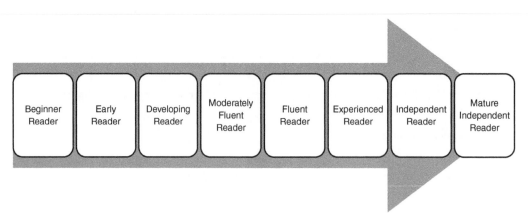

Figure 10.2   Version of the CLPE Reading scales.

Formative Assessment of Reading at KS2

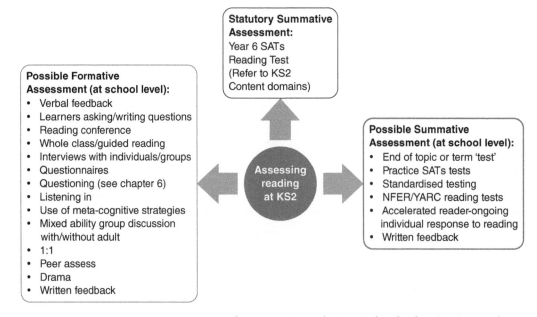

Figure 10.3   Assessing comprehension in a Key Stage 2 class

Outside of the statutory assessment requirements, formative assessment is what drives effective teaching. In Black and Wiliam's research (2010), they suggest the classroom is like a black box; on the outside are the elements such as parents, pupils, teachers, policies (local and global) and resources which are all fed into the box and aim to produce successful learners. Of course, these elements change all the time due to the nature of the cohort, budgets, and government policy. Therefore, they say, what goes on *inside* the box, the teacher's formative assessment of the individual, is what really matters. Teachers can assess pupils and modify the teaching to enhance the progress of an individual. In planning for progression in comprehension, formative assessment is vital.

Figure 10.3 shows possible formative assessment strategies that might be used for assessing comprehension. The remainder of this chapter will focus on how those strategies might be used with challenging texts to assess depth of comprehension.

Method of assessment:

- Mixed ability discussion

- Using key verbs from the content domain to form questions

- Listening in

CASE STUDY

National Curriculum Year 5 and 6: *drawing inferences such as inferring characters' feelings, thoughts, and motives from their actions, and justifying inferences with evidence. (DfE, 2013)*

The importance of text choice for developing higher level readers is clear (chapter 3) as is the use of questioning (chapter 6). Mo regularly used starter activities to invite discussion using question prompts from the content domain. He had been reading *The Boy Who Swam With Piranhas* by David Almond to his year 6 class; a quirky, funny book about Stanley Potts, a boy who runs away to join the circus, but with lots of layers inviting discussion about the key themes of identity, mental health, and truth.

The following slide was displayed for the children to discuss (Figure 10.4). (Resource by Sharon Lannie)

Mo allowed ten minutes for the children to discuss their answers. His class were seated in mixed ability groups and he regularly moved pupils around to work with different peers. This activity enabled children to discuss up to four areas relating to the passage (although often he would use

(Continued)

(Continued)

pictures or film clips rather than text). Mo's ethos was built upon The Matthew Effect (Stanovich, 1986. See chapter 9), and the belief that mixed ability groupings meant that everyone benefited from either hearing new ideas they may not have thought about, or sharing examples from experience or embedding their own learning through explanation. He was also aware that children are often 'braver' when discussing in small groups which would enhance critical literacy. Mo's observations also confirmed that if the children's discussion deviated from the original question, it was usually relevant to the themes or ideas around the text; again those 'layers' that encourage children to explore their own interpretations, leading to a deeper comprehension.

Infer
What is the policeman's attitude towards Stan and 'the fairground folk'?

'The Boy Who Swam With Piranhas' by David Almond

Explain:
What do you think the writer wants you to think about?

As Stan and the fairground workers arrive in town to set up the fair, a policeman stops them.

"I know lads like you and I know what lads like you get up to, 'specially in these dark days. In fact, I know all you ragamuffin fairground folk traipsing and wandering across the world and leaving all kinds of bother in your wake. I also know that if I had my way..."he lowers the torch "But that's another tale."(p85)

Compare:
Does this remind you of any news stories where groups of people have been treated like this?

Writer's choice:
Why does the writer use ellipses here?

In terms of assessment, Mo would 'listen in' from a distance and note pupils who could engage and look more deeply into a text. He would also be able to identify those who needed support to look more critically and those that 'led' or 'challenged'. He would use this information to identify any issues that required attention, from a social or inclusive point of view as well as to identify gaps in learning. In this case, as expected, conversation related to a recent incident where a group of Travellers had moved to a park near the school and were eventually evicted. Mo was able to gauge the 'feeling' around this and link it back to the character Stan for further discussion.

Case study reflections:

- Are there opportunities for your pupils to explore each other's ideas and reflect on their own ideas and values?
- How is talk structured and how do you assess that meaningfully?
- How do you ensure that all pupils feel their contributions are valued?

Method of assessment: Children generating questions

National Curriculum Year 5 and 6: *discuss and evaluate how authors use language, including figurative language, considering the impact on the reader.*

CASE STUDY:

During a whole class reading session, Anayah's Year 5 class had all been introduced to the poem *New Moon* (see Figure 1) through Kate Wakeling's video reading (see https://www.clpe.org.uk/files/kate-wakeling-new-moon). Wakeling introduces the poem as 'a poem about the very, very first, very, very small bit of moon that you might see'.

Harvey and Logan were both 'good' readers in the sense of decoding and independence. Their task was to write three questions which would encourage the reader to look at Wakeling's use of language and why (they felt) she had chosen certain words. They also had to give some possible answers (see the conversation between Harvey and Logan below).

New Moon

Moon is
silver sliver.

Moon is
clipped cup
from which to sip
a first drop
of freshly-pressed
moon juice.

Moon is
somersaulting C
in the best moon font.

Moon is fickle flickerer.

Moon is
new lunar lantern
to track a star or two.

But mostly,
moon is
shy to meet
once more
that
old old
sky.

From '*Moonjuice*' by Wakeling (2016)

H: Ok, I noticed that the language was very similar - lots of sounds repeated like 's' and 'c', but I'm not sure why.

L: Like 'silver sliver'? She (the poet) said it was the tiny beginning of the moon, I can picture it. You know, when it is only just the tiny edge of the circle.

(Continued)

(Continued)

H: That is why she has used the word 'sliver'; like a tiny bit of glass. And it goes well with silver because that's alliteration and, well, it's almost the same word as 'silver'.

L: So, we could ask 'Why has Wakeling described the moon as 'silver silver''?

H: Ok, so what would the answer be?

L: Something like...because it looks like the tiniest bit of silver, and she's used alliteration because...hmmm...

H: Because it sounds quiet? And it's always quiet at that time when the moon's out? You can't even say it loud, can you? (They both try it.)

L: Maybe we can also ask where else she has used alliteration? There are loads of examples. (They point to a few.) Ok, so they could give a few possibilities.

H: Ok, what else do you notice? What about 'What is a fickle flickerer'? I'm not sure what it is? What does 'fickle' mean? Pass me the dictionary. (They look it up.) Ok, it means 'changeable' or 'inconsistent'. A 'changing flickerer'? Something that changes and flickers? Does it mean flicker like a candle? Like on and off?

L: Well, moon is light as well. It sparkles. Yes, I think so. So, we could ask, 'What do you think a 'fickle flickerer is'...

H: ...and the answer should be, something that sparkles in and out; it flickers and changes, like a candle. Like the stars really, except that she has used alliteration again to give it that soft sound and make it sound sort of more magical than 'the moon sparkles'.

L: Ok, so our three questions are:

1. 'Why has Wakeling described the moon as 'silver silver''?
2. Can you find an example of alliteration?
3. Why is the moon called a 'fickle flickerer'?

CASE STUDY REFLECTIONS

Anayah could see that from the three questions and answers the boys had formulated, they were able to meet the objective; they had been able to work together to reflect and understand the meaning of the poem and also how the poet's use of language contributed to that.

- Could this method of questioning be used with any text?
- Consider how you provide opportunities for children to discuss and share their ideas which are not dependent on written answers.
- Consider your pairing - would it work better for mixed ability or similar ability?

Method of assessment - Listening in

As Harvey and Logan were working independently, Anayah relied on the outcome of the written questions to assess the boys against the learning objective. Another method would have been to have 'listened in'. From looking at the dialogue between the boys above, the depth of conversation around putting the questions together is especially interesting and shows that both boys are more than able to independently find the meaning of words (finding 'fickle' in the dictionary); apply the meaning to the context ('like a candle') and explore depth of meaning ('Because it sounds quiet? And it's always quiet at that time when the moon's out? You can't even say it loud, can you?'). Listening in, as a technique, offers the opportunity to hear the process behind the conclusion; a glimpse into the meta-cognition needed to access 'deeper' understanding. Of course, this may not be practical for a teacher to always assess in this way, but when this is done well, it can be very incisive and feedback could be instant.

Reading comprehension and meta-cognition

Meta-cognition, the process by which you think about what you are thinking, is the key to becoming a highly skilled reader (Afflerbach *et al*, 2013). Paris & Winograd (1990) explained that meta-cognition awareness was instrumental for high levels of comprehension and that 'good comprehenders' were aware of, and could manipulate, the strategies needed to enhance their reading. Largely, if we are focusing on our higher-level readers, then meta-cognition, the skill of monitoring your own comprehension process, is crucial (Klingner, 2004; Afflerbach, 2016). In terms of assessment, teachers should be able to identify those pupils who are meta-cognitively aware and develop those that are not.

The questions in Figure 10.5 were part of the Metacognitive Awareness of Reading Strategies Inventory (MARSI) (Mokhtari & Reichard, 2002) used to explore a group of students' awareness of the strategies they used to comprehend a text.

1. I have a purpose in mind when I read.
2. I take notes while reading to help me understand what I'm reading.
3. I think about how to be a high-level reader, what I know to help me understand what I'm reading.
4. I preview the text to see what it's about before reading it.
5. When text becomes difficult, I read aloud to help me understand what I'm reading.
6. I write summaries to reflect on key ideas in the text.
7. I think about whether the content of the text fits my purpose.
8. I read slowly but carefully to be sure I understand what I'm reading.
9. I discuss my reading with others to check my understanding.

(Continued)

(Continued)

10. I skim the text first by noting characteristics like length and organization.
11. I try to get back on track when I lose concentration.
12. I underline or circle information in the text to help me remember it.
13. I adjust my reading speed according to what I'm reading.
14. I decide what to read closely and what to ignore.
15. I use reference materials such as dictionaries to help me understand what I'm reading.
16. When text becomes difficult, I begin to pay closer attention to what I'm reading.
17. I use tables, figures, and pictures in text to increase my understanding.
18. I stop from time to time to think about what I'm reading.
19. I use context clues to help me better understand what I'm reading.
20. I paraphrase (restate ideas in my own words) to better understand what I'm reading.
21. I try to picture or visualize information to help me remember what I'm reading.
22. I use typographical aids like boldface type and italics to identify key information.
23. I critically analyse and evaluate the information presented in the text.
24. I go back and forth in the text to find relationships among ideas in it.
25. I check my understanding when I come across conflicting information.
26. I try to guess what the text is about when reading.
27. When text becomes difficult, I reread to increase my understanding.
28. I ask myself questions I like to have answered in the text.
29. I check to see if my guesses about the text are right or wrong.
30. I try to guess the meaning of unknown words or phrases.

Figure 10.5   The Metacognitive Awareness of Reading Strategies Inventory (MARSI)

It is not a suggestion to give these 30 questions to the class, but rather, in terms of assessment, teachers could model themselves using these meta-cognitive strategies and also look for evidence of the strategies being used by more independent readers.

CASE STUDY: METHOD OF ASSESSMENT: META-COGNITION STRATEGIES

National Curriculum Year 5 and 6: *to explain and discuss your understanding of what you have read.*

Ross modelled this process to his year 5 class during whole class reading. In introducing the first chapter of Welford's 'The 1000-year-old boy', he modelled how he made sense of the extract.

Below is a transcript of the lesson:

Ross: I'm going to read the opening of the text. I know the beginning is important as it can give me a lot of information about the characters and the story. Ok... (He reads it aloud to the class).

Alfie

Would you like to live forever? I am afraid I cannot recommend it. I am used to it now, and I do understand how special it is. Only I want to stop now. I want to grow up like you. This is my story. My name is Alve Einarsson. I am a thousand years old. More, actually. Are we friends? In that case, just call me Alfie. Alfie Monk. (Extract from The 1000-Year-Old Boy by Welford, R, p5)

Ross: Ok...I don't know about you but that seemed like a lot of unusual information! Is it about a boy who is actually 1000 years old? I need to re-read it, to check. He reads again. This time he stops and 'says outloud' his thoughts, articulating the strategies he is using to interpret the text (Afflerbach *et al*, 2015). Figure 10.6 demonstrates this.

Modelling meta-cognition-strategies used by Ross	Parts of the text referred to	Assessment opportunities: possible behaviour demonstrated by students using the strategy
Stopping from time to time to think about what has been read.	Throughout the extract.	• Seen when reading 1:1 or group. • Saying aloud the meaning in their own words • Reads expecting to understand the text
Critically analysing and evaluating the information presented in the text. Eg: "I think that would be great?" "Does that mean the character has tried it?"	Would you like to live forever? I am afraid I cannot recommend it.	• Answering the questions • Debating the issues • Reflecting on the 'answers' given in the text • Responding to partners' viewpoints

(Continued)

(Continued)

Modelling meta-cognition-strategies used by Ross	Parts of the text referred to	Assessment opportunities: possible behaviour demonstrated by students using the strategy
Asking questions you would like to have answered in the text. Eg: "Why does he want to stop? I wonder if he does stop?"	I am used to it now, and I do understand how special it is. Only I want to stop now. I want to grow up like you.	• Commenting on events/themes • Commenting when questions are answered, or more crop up.
Re-reading the text twice to clarify tricky words. "Alve Einarsson. Alve Einarsson? That's unusual. Maybe it's not English?"	This is my story. My name is Alve Einarsson. I am a thousand years old. More, actually.	• Repeating words • Discussing the meaning • Understands there is a problem and looks for ways round this
Asking questions that need clarifying. "He must be the main character. The boy who is 1000 years old? Will he stop like he wants to?"	Are we friends? In that case, just call me Alfie. Alfie Monk.	• Discussing questions and answering them • Refining them and reflecting regularly to form new ones.

Figure 10.6   Modelling and assessing meta-cognitive strategies

Assessment strategy: Focus group discussion

Whilst most of the class worked in pairs to read and discuss the next section of the book, Ross worked with a focus group of six children (also in pairs), to read the next part of the chapter together (using the same learning objective). As he observed, the group read the text and worked in pairs to verbalise their understanding. He made notes of strategies that were used. After several minutes, the group reconvened and Ross initiated the dialogue around the understanding of the text, focusing his questions on strategies used as well as pupils' answers: for example, what the children did when they got to a tricky part, which part they needed to re-read and what questions had they asked during the course of the discussion. He used his observations to make the strategy explicit for the reader and to demonstrate to the others his thought processes; or example: "I noticed you went back to the first bit, Mabel, to check the characters' names. Why did you do that?"

Case study reflections

• How do you verbalise your meta-cognitive strategies when modelling reading?

• How do you provide opportunities to have a dialogue with pupils about why they use certain strategies?

• Could you focus on a group and assess only for the meta-cognitive strategies used?

Assessment and teacher workload

Teachers should always be mindful of the tasks set and the amount of work generated by that task which may need written feedback (marking). Marking is of course a method of assessment, but assessment does not always mean marking, which is an important distinction. For example, the written answers to the questions about 'The Executioner's Daughter', earlier in this chapter, were used as a written summative task, possibly to measure where the reader 'is' at the end of a term. Presumably, 30 children completing the same task could easily be an evening's marking, if the expectation was to annotate a pupil's work and give 'next steps'. However, teachers and support staff could also use the same questions in small group discussion; making notes of the responses and encouraging deeper thinking through questioning and giving children instant feedback. Consider children also 'writing in pairs'. Can they answer the questions together; therefore collaborating and agreeing through discussion? This would also reduce any written feedback by half.

That is not to say written feedback should not happen, only that teachers should be mindful that there is no evidence that extensive comments and using different coloured pens have a positive effect on progress (DfE, 2016; EEF, 2016). Ofsted are also keen to highlight that there is no expectation for schools to use writing/written feedback for every lesson to 'prove' progress (DfE, 2018); instead all marking should be 'meaningful, motivating, and manageable' and should be used to advance pupil progress (DfE, 2018, p8).

Conclusion

Assessment of reading must be a combination of methods. Of course, schools will want to prepare pupils for the Key Stage 2 SATs reading test. However, to move your readers forward, towards the goal of reading widely and independently, for purpose and for pleasure, teachers need to ensure they know what this success looks like; the steps needed for the individual to get there; that those steps are modelled and structured and that pupils have the widest range of relevant reading material needed alongside this.

CHAPTER SUMMARY

This chapter explores the assessment of reading at all levels. From statutory requirements to formative assessment, teachers should consider pupils' individual reading attainment; where pupils need to go next and how pupils can be supported to do so. The chapter includes some practical strategies to support teachers with assessment of reading, alongside observations of what successful reading looks like. There is also a focus on workload; it is essential that teachers realise that marking is not the only way to assess and make use of the many strategies suggested to assess children's reading.

Further reading

Familiarise yourself with the 'Eliminating unnecessary workload around marking agenda'. Available at : https://assets.publishing.service.gov.uk/government/uploads/system/uploads/attachment_data/file/511256/Eliminating-unnecessary-workload-around-marking.pdf

Education Endowment Foundation (EEF) (2018) *Preparing for Literacy*. London: DfE.

References

Afflerbach, P (2016) Reading assessment: Looking ahead. *The Reading Teacher 69*:4 p413–419.

Afflerbach, P. Byeong-Young, Cho., Jong-Yun, K., Elliker Crassas, M., Doyle, B (2013) Reading: What else matters besides strategies and skills? *The Reading Teacher. 66*:6, 440–448.

Afflerbach, Peter. Byeong-Young, Cho & Jong-Yun, Kim (2015) Conceptualizing and assessing higher-order thinking in reading. *Theory Into Practice. 54*:3, 203–212.

Almond, D (2012) *The Boy Who Swam with Piranhas.* London: Walker.

Black, P. and Wiliam, D. (2010) *Inside the Black Box. Raising Standards through Classroom Assessment. 92*:1. 81–90.

CLPE (2016) Reading Scales https://www.clpe.org.uk/sites/default/files/CLPE%20READING%20 SCALE%20REBRAND.pdf

Department for Education (DfE) (2013) *The National Curriculum in England: Framework document.* London: DfE.

Department for Education (DfE) (2016) *Eliminating unnecessary workload around marking: Report of the Independent Teacher Workload Review.* London DfE.

Department for Education (DfE) (2017a) Teacher assessment exemplification: KS2 English reading.

Department for Education (DfE) (2017b) Teacher assessment frameworks at the end of key stage 2 For use in the 2017 to 2018 academic year. London: DfE.

Department for Education (DfE) (2018) *Ofsted Inspections: myths.* London: DfE.

Education Endowment Foundation (EEF) (2016) *A Marked Improvement? A review of the evidence on written marking.* Oxford University: DfE.

Education Endowment Foundation (EEF) (2018) *Preparing for Literacy.* London: DfE.

Hardstaff, J. (2016) *The Executioner's Daughter.* London: Egmont.

Keenan, J. (2016) Assessing the assessments reading comprehension tests. *Perspectives on Language and Literacy. 42*:3 17–21.

Klingner, J. (2004) *Assessing Reading Comprehension. 29*:4. 59–70.

Mokhtari, K and Reichard, C. (2002) Assessing students' metacognitive awareness of reading strategies. *Journal of Educational Psychology. 94*:2. 249–259.

Paris, S. G., and Winograd, P. (1990). How metacognition can promote academic learning and instruction. Cited in B. F. Jones & L. Idol (Eds.), *Dimensions of Thinking and Cognitive Instruction.* p15–51. Hillsdale, NJ: Erlbaum.

Snowling, M., Cain, K., Nation, K., & Oakhill, J.(2009) *Reading comprehension: nature, assessment and teaching. Assessment for effective intervention. 29*:4.

STA (2015) *Interim assessment framework* https://www.gov.uk/government/publications/teacher-assessment-framework-at-the-end-of-key-stage-2

STA (2018) *2018 teacher assessment guidance: key stage 2* http://www.gov.uk/government/publications/2018-teacher-assessment-guidance-key-stage-2

STA, (2016) The KS2 content domain https://www.gov.uk/government/publications/key-stage-2-english-reading-test-framework

Stanovich, K.E. (1986) Matthew effects in reading: some consequences of individual differences in the acquisition of literacy. *Reading Research Quarterly. 21*:360–406.

Wakeling, K. (2016) *Moonjuice.* Birmingham: The Emma Press Ltd.

Welford, R. (2018) *The 1000-Year-Old Boy.* London: Harper-Collins.

11
BUILDING A READING CULTURE

— CHAPTER OBJECTIVES —

This chapter will allow you to achieve the following outcomes:

- Understand the importance of the learning environment when teaching reading comprehension;
- Consider ways in which you can build a reading culture within your classroom.

— LINKS TO THE TEACHERS' STANDARDS —

Working through this chapter will help you meet the following standards:

2. Promote good progress and outcomes by pupils

3. Demonstrate good subject and curriculum knowledge

5. Adapt teaching to respond to the strengths and needs of all pupils

Introduction

The final chapter of this book is designed to build on the previous chapters and capture the essence of what makes an effective reading culture. The book focuses on how best to support and challenge those pupils working at a high level of comprehension and how we can develop this further to ensure that pupils are working at greater depth. Assessment is key to ensuring children develop into lifelong readers and each chapter has outlined ways in which pupils are assessed to secure breadth and depth of knowledge and understanding.

It is important that class teachers continue to engage with recent and relevant research around reading comprehension in order to make informed decisions around the most effective way to teach reading. Throughout this book, we have used research to underpin professional practice and have drawn on pedagogical innovations through case studies which demonstrate real impact upon learners. When considering your own practice, it may be useful to identify what it is that inspires and motivates your class of readers. Choice of texts, book groups, engagement with authors and an inviting reading environment all contribute to building a culture of reading, and while we have written a book specifically to address the needs of those children with higher levels of comprehension skills, we are aware that everything in this book may be applied to all pupils to some extent. We have sought to include a wide variety of information which will enable you, as the class teacher, to situate the learning within your own contextual framework.

ACTIVITY

Consider your own classroom practice in light of previous chapters and make notes on how you already address the teaching of comprehension skills.

- Does your classroom promote reading for pleasure?
- Do you use a thematic approach to teaching texts?
- Have you a range of challenging texts on display?
- How do you facilitate reading conferences?
- How does your assessment identify gaps in learning?
- How does your planning identify key questions designed to challenge thinking?
- Are you developing and building upon critical thinking skills? In what ways?

These questions are crucial when defining your own practice and careful attention to each will undoubtedly enhance practice further. They allow for reflection within a busy classroom and by answering these you will be able to focus your teaching to ensure progression in learning.

Classroom environment

The physical environment

This encompasses not only the furniture, layout and texts within the book area, but also the teacher as a reader. You are instrumental in ensuring the environment is conducive to developing a lifelong love of books and reading. Your actions, attitude and enthusiasm will all have an influence on the children within your class in terms of their journey as a reader. We can all remember that one teacher who inspired us to read more widely or the one who suggested a book which became a firm favourite. Think back to when you listened to a teacher read from a class novel. How did they hold your attention? How did they engage with the audience? Did they encourage opinions and discussion around plot, character, themes and settings?

I remember advising a Year 5 colleague to read *Stig of the Dump* by Clive King with their class as a whole-class text around which a range of writing opportunities could take place. A few weeks into the book, she came to see me because the children were not 'connecting' with the text and the level of engagement that she expected from her pupils was not progressing as she would have wished. When exploring this further, it was evident that my colleague did not have the same amount of enthusiasm for *Stig* as I had demonstrated. I had vivid memories of reading this myself and had channelled this into my suggestions for Year 5. This was a critical moment within my own professional practice and led to my setting up a book club for teachers whereby for five minutes at the beginning of a staff meeting, we could share our favourite children's book or introduce colleagues to new and exciting authors. Listening to teachers discuss their favourite texts from their own childhood as well as sharing more recent reads led to a great deal of what we termed 'book gossip'.

Teresa Cremin's ongoing research around 'Teachers as Readers' (Cremin *et al*, 2009) makes explicit the importance of teachers engaging with books in a meaningful and knowledgeable manner. The project found that teachers relied heavily on a narrow canon of children's authors when teaching reading in school. By working with schools and teachers, the project encouraged teachers to widen their repertoire of children's books and authors so as to ensure pupils had access to a wide range of diverse texts. From this a number of teachers' reading groups were set up across the country on a much larger scale than my school-based 'book gossip' sessions where teachers could come together to share their knowledge of children's authors. With the growth of Twitter over the last few years, it is easy to set up an online community where that love of reading can be shared and where this can be used to develop children's engagement and motivation.

CASE STUDY

This case study illustrates how the use of social media, in particular Twitter, was used to engage readers in the classroom.

Sara was teaching in Year 4 and was keen to further enhance pupils' critical literacy through the use of focused pupil conferences. She was an avid user of Twitter as a professional development tool and regularly engaged with online reading groups. One of the books recommended for engaging and inspiring readers was *Brightstorm* by Vashti Hardy. Although not exceptionally challenging in terms of lexical density, grammatical complexity and vocabulary (Fang and Pace, 2013), Sara could see how the plot, characters and themes would challenge her advanced readers in terms of their understanding. Careful questioning drawing upon Barretts taxonomy (1968) enabled Sara to encourage a deeper level of thinking when exploring characters' motives. Arthur and Maudie Brightstorm's actions throughout the course of the story were interrogated and pupils working within her book group were able to discuss this with reference to evidence gleaned from previous chapters. As such, they were able to make appropriate predictions and suggestions as to how the story might move forward.

(Continued)

(Continued)

Sara followed Vashti Hardy on Twitter and was able to ask questions which came directly from her pupils – these were then shared by screenshotting so that pupils were able to access Vashti's feedback. This provided pupils with a different perspective when considering authorial intent. As an aside, Vashti Hardy regularly tweets about other children's books which she is reading which demonstrated to Sara's pupils that even though Vashti was a published author in her own right, she still read other novels and championed books by other authors. This was so important for developing a culture of reading within Sara's classroom.

In a staff development workshop, Sara was able to share this practice with colleagues and demonstrate the impact that this had upon pupil attainment and motivation. Pupils had written detailed character studies of Arthur and Maudie in response to Sara's questions; however, due to interaction with the author, these were more analytical, examining motives rather than listing characteristics. Her pupils were eager for Vashti Hardy's next novel to be published and let her know via Twitter!

Below are some key people and organisations to follow if you are keen to extend your own knowledge of children's books and authors.

@BarringtonStoke

@BooksForKeeps

@booksfortopics

@Booktrust

@clpe1

@FlyingEyeBooks

@hodderchildrens

@imaginecentre

@KidsBloomsbury

@lit4pleasure

@Literacy_Trust

@louisebeattie10

@MarilynBrock

@Mat_at_Brookes

@NATEfeed

@nikkigamble

@NosyCrow

@orchardbooks

@patronofreading

@PenguinUKBooks

@PrimarySchoolBC

@PuffinBooks

@readingagency

@RGladiators

@scottishbktrust

@sharonlannie

@suzannehorton11

@TeresaCremin

@TinyOwl_books

@Uklaureate

@WalkerBooksUK

These are just a few of the publishers, organisations, charities and individuals that tweet about all things reading. There are also many children's authors that are on Twitter who are more than happy to engage with their readers in this manner. In this day and age, where instant gratification is the norm, Twitter provides an up-to-date, immediate forum which allows teachers to have those discussions around reading for pleasure which may enhance their own knowledge and understanding and that of their pupils.

A shared ethos

Many classrooms foster a love of books and reading which permeates throughout the school and into the wider community but what does this look like in terms of ethos? Raising the profile of reading within your school is key to achieving greater engagement which in turn will lead to increased attainment, evident in the research conducted within this area (Clark and de Zoysa, 2011; Petscher 2010, Twist *et al.*, 2007).

Questions to ask yourself might include:

- How do you choose your class texts?

- Do pupils suggest suitable books and authors?

- How does what you are reading impact upon your class?

- How do you share this with other classes and teachers in school?

- Would your pupils describe you as a reading teacher?

Research has shown that as pupils transition from primary to secondary school, they are less likely to read for pleasure. Indeed, Clark and Teravainen (2017), in their recent study of 42,406 children and young adults aged between 8 and 18, found that in 2016, the percentage of pupils aged 8–11 who stated that they did not enjoy reading at all was 3.6 per cent. This rose to 8–9 per cent for pupils aged 11–14, with a further rise to 14.9 per cent for pupils aged 14–16. It therefore appears that, by building a reading culture among our Key Stage 2 primary pupils, we are more likely to ensure that this is continued into Key Stage 3 and 4 where subject content within the National Curriculum talks of developing *an appreciation and love of reading* while encouraging pupils to *read increasingly challenging material independently* (DfE, 2014, p.15).

Considering this in terms of our advanced readers, it is clear that developing skills of comprehension at a high level will stand pupils in good stead as they begin their secondary education. Involving pupils in this choice and ensuring that teachers promote challenging yet appropriate texts will reinforce a positive reading ethos. If pupils have already had the opportunity to read *a wide range of fiction … including in particular whole books, short stories, poems and plays with a wide coverage of genres, historical periods, forms and authors*, they should be more open to *choosing and reading books independently for challenge, interest and enjoyment* (DfE, 2014, p15).

Assessment

Assessment and its place within a reading classroom can influence how pupils perceive reading. If reading comprehension is associated with reading extracts from texts or short stories and answering pre-determined questions, we might lose sight of the important place of talk when developing skills of inference, deduction, prediction and analysis. The benefits of peer group discussion have long been highlighted through research when considering how collaborative talk can enhance learning (Alexander, 2004; Mercer, 2000).

Black and Wiliam's powerful research around formative assessment revealed how this type of assessment, when conducted within a supportive environment, could potentially accelerate learning gain for individual pupils (Black and Wiliam, 1998). If we consider the needs of our advanced readers, it is imperative that we do not place a ceiling upon their learning, neither do we blindly chase objectives derived from the Key Stage 3 subject content within the national curriculum. Formative assessment will allow the teacher to direct discussions, scaffold learning and introduce higher-level thinking skills in a timely manner. According to Wiliam and Thompson (2008), formative assessment may be implemented in short-, medium- and long-term cycles. So, what does this look like in terms of developing comprehension skills? Consider Table 11.1.

Table 11.1   Formative assessment – short-, medium- and long-term cycles

Assessment cycle	Interaction	Assessment ideas
Short term	Pupil – pupil Teacher – pupil	• Self or peer assessment • Targeted questions from the teacher which re-shape discussion • Verbal feedback • Explanation of vocabulary within context
Medium term	Pupil – teacher	• Questions posed to groups of readers • Written answers • Responses to texts • Mapping diagrams
Long term	Teacher – class/ group	• Breadth of reading • Attitude to reading

Although attitudes to reading and breadth of reading material may be more complex in terms of assessment, they are nevertheless important in ensuring that pupils move on in their learning. Secure knowledge of your pupils and their reading development will allow planning to address any gaps in learning. When considering those pupils who are already demonstrating that they are ready to move on, you may want to ensure that they are able to reflect upon their own learning and are ready to actively engage with constructing their own knowledge and understanding; by doing so you will not only be meeting Teachers' Standard 2c – *guide pupils to reflect on the progress they have made and their emerging needs* (DfE, 2012, p10) – but also contributing to building a reading culture.

LEARNING OUTCOMES REVIEW

In this chapter, we have explored how important it is to build a reading culture within your classroom and your school. You should also be aware of how assessment can be used effectively to support, extend and challenge readers in terms of reading comprehension. The process of developing higher-level readers is not an easy one and does not simply happen because they are reading widely. Your responsibility as the class teacher is to nurture this so as to ensure they are pre-pared for the demands of a secondary curriculum and that they are able to champion reading as a positive and respected pastime. If pupils value the process and continue to think critically about the texts they encounter, they are much more likely to have a broader understanding of the world around them. Skills of analysis, synthesis, evaluation, reflection and criticality will be deepened through comprehensive teaching of texts and their place within our society.

Further reading

Hall, K (2003) *Listening to Stephen Read: Multiple perspectives on literacy.* Buckingham: Open University Press.

This book offers many perspectives on reading drawn from the responses of reading experts. It is steeped in rigorous research which supports the teaching of reading using a variety of approaches.

Saunders, L (2015) *Progression in Primary English.* London: Sage.

The chapter on reading comprehension provides a detailed overview of theory and research around teaching reading. It explores pedagogical knowledge while allowing the reader to reflect upon their own professional practice.

References

Alexander, R (2004) *Towards dialogic teaching: Rethinking classroom talk.* York: Dialogos UK.

Barrett, TC (1968) Taxonomy of cognitive and affective dimensions of reading comprehension, in T Clymer (ed.) *What is 'reading?' Some current concepts.* Chicago: University of Chicago Press.

Black, P and Wiliam, D (1998) Assessment and classroom learning, *Assessment in Education: Principles, Policy and Practice, 5* (1): 7–74.

Clark, C and De Zoysa, S (2011) *Mapping the interrelationships of Reading Enjoyment, attitudes, behaviour and attainment: An exploratory investigation.* London: National Literacy Trust.

Clark, C and Teravainen, A (2017) *Celebrating Reading for Enjoyment: Findings from our Annual Literacy Survey 2016.* London: National Literacy Trust.

Cremin, T, Mottram, M, Collins, F, Powell, S and Safford, K (2009) Teachers as readers: Building communities of readers, *Literacy, 43* (1): 11–19.

Department for Education (DfE) (2012) *Teachers' standards,* **http://webarchive.nationalarchives. gov.uk/20130404065617/https://www.education.gov.uk/publications/eOrdering-Download/teachers%20standards.pdf**

Department for Education (DfE) (2013) *Teachers' Standards.* Available at **www.education.gov.uk**

Department for Education (DfE) (2014) *The National Curriculum in England: Key Stages 3 and 4: Framework document.* London: DfE.

Fang, Z and Pace, BG (2013) Teaching with challenging texts in the disciplines: text complexity and close reading, *Journal of Adolescent and Adult Literacy, 57* (2): 104–8.

Hardy, V (2018) *Brightstorm*. London: Scholastic Children's Books.

King, C (1963) *Stig of the Dump*. London: Penguin Books.

Mercer, N (2000) *Words and Minds: How we use language to think together*. London: Routledge.

Petscher, Y (2010) A meta-analysis of the relationship between student attitudes towards reading and achievement in reading, *Journal of Research in Reading, 33* (4): 335–55.

Twist, L, Schagan, I and Hogson, C (2007) *Progress in International Reading Literacy Study (PIRLS): Reader and Reading National Report for England 2006*. Slough: NFER.

Wiliam, D and Thompson, M (2008) Integrating assessment with instruction: What will it take to make it work? In CA Dwyer (ed.) *The Future of Assessment: Shaping teaching and learning*. New York: Lawrence Erlbaum Associates, pp53–82.

INDEX